Berlitz®
Australia

Front cover: majestic Uluru (Ayers Rock)

Right: kangaroos are a common sight in the bush

TOP 10 ATTRACTIONS

Great Ocean Road This coastal drive offers some truly spectacular views *(page 179)*

Kakadu National Park Home to giant termite mounds and ancient Aboriginal art *(page 107)*

Barossa Valley Australia's best-known wine-growing region is located in South Australia *(page 152)*

The Blue Mountains This dramatic region of forested ravines and pristine bush is just west of Sydney *(page 62)*

Sydney • Home to Australia most iconic architectu *(page 3*

Uluru Also known as Ayers Rock, this enormous sandstone monolith has been venerated by the local Aboriginal peoples for centuries *(page 115)*

Perth A stylish and vibrant modern metropolis *(page 125)*

Unique wildlife Encounter kangaroos, koalas, wombats and crocodiles in their natural habitat *(page 10)*

Great Barrier Reef Located off the Queensland coast, it is one of the natural wonders of the world *(page 86)*

Melbourne An elegant and sophisticated city *(page 162)*

CONTENTS

196

118

211

66

193

33

Features

INTRODUCTION

Australia is a vast place. The country covers an entire continent of about 7.68 million square km (2.97 million sq miles) – about the same size as the United States excluding Alaska and Hawaii. That's big enough to have several distinct climates – from cool temperate to monsoonal – and three time zones. The natural landscapes are correspondingly diverse, ranging from red deserts to green rainforests and from sandy beaches to snow-clad mountains. Natural beauty is complemented by sophisticated cities, where all the pleasures of urban life are at hand – usually with beaches and national parks on the doorstep.

Aussie Stereotypes

Perhaps it's because of this size and diversity, together with its isolation, that for most of its history, Australia has been little known and even less understood. A character in an Oscar Wilde play set in the Victorian era summed up the foreigner's blurred impression of Australia: 'It must be so pretty with all the dear little kangaroos flying about. Agatha has found it on the map.'

> **The open door**
>
> In 1922, the novelist D.H. Lawrence wrote: 'Australia is like an open door with the blue beyond. You just walk out of the world and into Australia.'

In many people's minds the Land Down Under still consists of vague images: the Sydney Opera House, Bondi beach, the Great Barrier Reef, the unforgiving Outback, and all those bizarre Australian animals. It's true that the kangaroo, the koala, the wombat, the platypus and the Tasmanian devil exist nowhere else in the world outside zoos –

A lifeguard surveys the South Bank beach, Brisbane

An Aussie bushman

and neither does anything resembling them. But there is, of course, much more to the country than this.

And what of the human population? Australians tend to be perceived as a laid-back bunch, fond of sun-bathing, surfing and swilling cold beer. And there are the Australian 'types': a stockman herding sheep beneath eucalytus trees, or a tanned bushman prospecting in the stark landscape of the Outback. Like most clichés, there's something to it. Most Aussies (pronounced 'ozzies') relish the outdoor life. Many radiate health and either possess or admire tanned muscles. If they're not actually at the beach, Aussies are likely to be hiking, jogging, playing sport (or at least listening to football or cricket on the radio), or they are out in the garden barbecuing beef or seafood. To complete the picture, there's usually an icy beer at hand to pacify the fiercest thirst. Australians may not be the world's most insatiable beer drinkers, but they're high in the league.

Prospectors seeking gold, opals or other minerals still roam the Outback, the remote, sparsely inhabited back country of Australia's interior, typified by the town of Broken Hill *(see page 68)*. In Australia's wild northern 'Top End', enormous crocodiles stalk unwary prey, sometimes coming a little too close to civilisation – about 100 crocodiles a year are removed from Darwin's harbour. Remote cattle farms (called 'stations') are so big that stockmen conduct their roundups using helicopters. One of the stations is the size of Belgium.

However, these startling facts represent only part of the truth. Camping holidays or day-trips to national parks are as close as the overwhelming majority of Australians get to living in the bush. Australia is one of the world's most urbanised countries, with over 90 percent of its population living near the coast in the 10 biggest cities. More than one Australian in five resides in Sydney (population 4.3 million). Melbourne is approaching the same size, with half a million fewer inhabitants. Other state capitals – Brisbane, Adelaide and Perth – account for most of the rest of the population.

Natural Wonders

For many people, Australia's natural wonders, its odd wildlife and its far-flung open spaces still eclipse everything else. The vast and starkly beautiful Outback holds an almost hypnotic appeal. When the best-selling thriller author Stephen King took a short break from writing and roared into Australia's wide-open expanses on a motor-cycle, he described his sense of awe: 'If you stop, the silence is incredible. You feel very small; you can almost hear God breathing.' Bear in mind that you don't have to go as far as the Outback to find untouched nature. The Blue Mountains National Park, for example – a Unesco

Australia is a land of wide open spaces

A kangaroo with its joey

World Heritage Area – is only 90 minutes' drive from central Sydney.

Some extraordinary wildlife wanders the continent. Australia has a virtual monopoly on monotremes, mammals that lay eggs. Among them are the waddling, spine-covered echidna and the platypus, a half-aquatic furry mammal with a duck-like beak.

Rather more familiar are the continent's marsupials, equipped with pouches to solve the baby-sitting problem. Bounding across the landscape are numerous varieties of mocropods ('big feet'), from small wallabies to giant red kangaroos. Another marsupial, the languid, furry koala, eschews violent exercise, spending its days drowsing in the branches in a eucalyptus-induced haze. Its relative, the wombat – another vegetarian marsupial – prefers to burrow under stumps or logs, or in the banks of creeks. More commonly seen are possums, tree-dwelling marsupials that have colonised many suburban backyards, causing householders sleepless nights with their noisy nocturnal wanderings.

Birdwatchers here can count hundreds of species. Thrillingly colourful birds, such as the rainbow lorrikeet, are as common as sparrows in other countries, and lyrical or humorous birdcalls provide every evening's country music. These indigenous stars have names such as flowerpecker, honeyeater and kookaburra, but the favourite bird of crossword puzzlers – the emu – can't sing or fly.

Unsurprisingly, Australia has some unique specialities in the reptile department, too, including 2-m (6-ft) goannas, exotic creatures like the frill-necked lizard and the bearded dragon, and the world's largest crocodile, the salt-water croc, or 'saltie'. For good measure, the island contains more species of venomous snake than anywhere else on earth.

A Continent Cut Off

Australia has been isolated from other continents since it split from the remnants of the southern super-continent, Gondwana, about 40 million years ago. Cut off from the evolutionary mainstream, plants and animals developed in ways that have engrossed generations of scientists and astounded thousands of ordinary tourists.

For countless millennia, the only humans sharing the continent with these animals were nomadic Aboriginal tribes. These first Australians are believed to have arrived from Asia, probably by boat, somewhere between 50,000 and 100,000 years ago. Australia's Aborigines lived within tribal boundaries they believed had been created by hero ancestors in a period called the Dreamtime. Aborigines built no permanent structures but lived in a manner that ensured their survival in an often harsh environment.

Their lives changed little until European explorers began arriving in the 17th

Australia's Aborigines are proud of their heritage

and 18th centuries. The colonial history of Australia began in 1770 when Captain James Cook landed on Australia's east coast and claimed all the territory he charted for King George III. Shortly after Cook's arrival, the British decided Australia was an ideal place to send convicts and in 1787, Britain dispatched a fleet of soldiers and convicts to colonise Australia, one of the farthest-flung points of its Empire.

In a relatively short time, the British Empire had casually seized the traditional lands of Australia's hunter-gatherers. Aborigines were dispersed and massacred. Australia's indigenous people (who now represent about 2 percent of the country's population) did not gain the vote until 1962 and were not included in Australia's official census until 1967.

The fact that modern Australia can be traced back to chain gangs of convicted felons rather than to resolute idealists has left its mark on the national psyche, although the impact is fading. Australians were once notably defensive about their

The Commonwealth of Australia

Since 1901 the six former British colonies of Australia have been an independent federal commonwealth with a British-style parliamentary system. Apart from the six states, there are also two territories, the Australian Capital Territory (ACT) and the Northern Territory. Australia's Head of State is Queen Elizabeth II. She is represented by a Governor-General, who is nominated by the federal government and appointed by the Queen. The Prime Minister heads the federal government and is the leader of the party that holds the most seats in the lower chamber, the House of Representatives. The upper house is the Senate. The federal parliament is based in Canberra, a city founded in 1927. Like Washington DC, in the US, Canberra lies in its own administrative zone, the ACT. Each state and territory has its own government and leader, who is called the premier (states) or chief minister (territories).

country, asking foreigners what they thought of it, then waiting anxiously for the answer. These days, Aussies are more relaxed about such matters. The descendants of convicts have long since been outnumbered by the descendants of free settlers, but if Australians can prove convict ancestry they do so eagerly – it's considered a mark of prestige.

A kangaroo and emu support Australia's coat of arms

The country has much to be proud of. In little more than 200 years, a tiny European settlement founded in conditions of brutality, servitude and privation has prospered and transformed itself into a dynamic modern nation whose economy places it in the top 20 OECD countries in terms of gross domestic product. Tourism is one of the largest earners and a major employer, directly accounting for 460,000 jobs, or almost 5 percent of Australia's workforce.

Australia is a long way from northern-hemisphere population centres: 9,720km (6,000 miles) from the US and 17,820km (11,000 miles) from Britain. But non-stop or one-stop flights make the going relatively easy. More distant in cultural terms are Australia's nearest neighbours, Indonesia and Papua New Guinea, a kangaroo's hop to the north. The Asian connection is becoming more important, not only politically and economically, but in human terms; a look at the faces on any city street shows the vastly increased flow of immigrants from Southeast Asia.

Since the early 1980s, cultural intermingling has revolutionised the national diet. Urban Australia now enjoys a

Immigrant nation

In Australia, four out of 10 people are immigrants or the first-generation children of immigrants.

collage of culinary influences with fresh, high-quality ingredients. All the state capitals have lively café scenes and at least one nearby wine-growing area, giving the chance to sample wines at the cellar door. Climatic diversity allows Australia to produce both warm- and cool-climate wines and grow tropical fruit such as rambutans, custard apples, mangoes, coconuts and lychees, as well as strawberries, blackberries, apples, pears, oranges and mandarins.

In the capital cities, you'll have no trouble finding restaurants serving excellently prepared cuisine from as far afield as Thailand, Mexico, Cambodia, Japan, France, Hungary, Spain, Lebanon, Turkey or Italy. In smaller towns, the choice is more limited, and you may have to settle for a meat pie, fish and chips or chop suey.

Australia's geographical superlatives are clear-cut. It is the world's biggest island. More accurately, it is the smallest and least populous (about 20 million inhabitants) of the continents, and the only one housing a single nation. Australia measures about 4,000km (2,500 miles) east to west and 3,200km (2,000 miles) north to south. It is 24 times the area of the British Isles.

The Great Dividing Range, stretching almost the entire length of the eastern continent, and with a maxiumum elevation of just over 2,000m (6,500ft), separates a narrow fertile strip on the coast from the Outback. West of the range, the country becomes increasingly flat and dry. Habitation eventually ceases and – after thousands of kilometres – the horizon is broken only by occasional mysterious protuberances including Uluru (Ayers Rock) and Kata Tjuta (the Olgas), and starkly beautiful mountains such as the Flinders and Macdonnell ranges. Then, in the far south of Western Australia, a repeat of the mountain range-coastal strip pattern heralds the Indian Ocean.

While Outback Australia includes regions of breathtaking natural beauty, much of the interior is arid, consisting of immense deserts and salt pans. Only 7 percent of the country is arable, which is why the settlement pattern has been so different from that of the US, and why the population is so much smaller. Non-arable land is not necessarily unproductive: under the surface lie bauxite, coal, iron ore, copper, tin, silver, uranium, nickel, tungsten, lead, zinc, diamonds, natural gas and oil. Mining is one of Australia's biggest industries, accounting for 7 percent of the country's GDP.

Lush palm forest

A Variety of Vegetation

Australia is home to some of the world's best-preserved wilderness areas. The Unesco World Heritage List currently includes 15 Australian regions, ranging from the Great Barrier Reef and the Tasmanian Wilderness to the Wet Tropics of Queensland and Uluru–Kata Tjuta.

The rainforests of Australia, healthy, vast and diverse, form one of the world's best-preserved wilderness resources. From the lush, dense jungles of Tropical North Queensland, the rainforest region extends south to the planet's last great stand of temperate rainforest – the cool, moist forests of Tasmania. Apart from their sheer beauty, Australia's rainforests contain about half of all Australian plant species, including 'primitive' plant families providing direct links with the birth of flowering plants 100 million years ago.

At almost all Australian latitudes you'll see hardy trees of two main families. There are more than 600 species of flowering acacia (including the golden wattle from which Australia derives its national colours) and over 500 types of eucalyptus, ranging from low, stunted, scrub-like bushes to the great towering varieties of the highland forests. There are ghost gums, so-called because under the light of the moon they appear silvery-white, and rock-hard ironbarks, capable of blunting the toughest timber saws.

Australia is the world's flattest continent, although the nation's summit, Mt Kosciuszko (elevation 2,228m/7,308ft), is almost as high as Mexico City. You can ski in the Snowy Mountains from June to August. The country's first ski club, the Kiandra Snow-Shoe Club, was founded in 1870 – two years before the first clubs in the United States.

Australia is the driest continent, with only one river (the Murray) worthy of world ranking. The country's coastline of 36,735km (almost 23,000 miles) includes many sweeping empty beaches where you can see nobody for a whole day or longer. You can dip a toe, or a surfboard, in legendary waters, among them the Coral Sea, the Timor Sea, the Pacific Ocean, the Indian Ocean and the Southern Ocean.

The reef

The Great Barrier Reef is home to more than 1,500 species of fish as well as whales, dolphins, turtles and thousands of different crustaceans.

Underwater Wonders

Some of Australia's most colourful sights exist under the sea. Divers visit Australian waters to admire the

Snorkelling is a great way to explore the reef

sort of fish you see in a collector's tropical tank – only 10 times bigger. Gorgeous angel fish, clown anemone fish and moorish idols glide past the enthralled skin diver's mask. Big-mouthed sharks, sting rays and venomous scorpion fish may also be seen.

For enthusiasts of underwater spectacles, the most exciting place in the world is the Great Barrier Reef. This 1,944-km-(1,200-mile-) long miracle – a living structure of coral – thrills the imagination in its immensity and in the intricate detail of brightly hued organisms shaped like antlers, flowers, fans or brains. It's the world's largest living thing. The most sublime tropical fish congregate here, too.

The reef, one of Australia's top tourist destinations, has become ever more accessible. So has Uluru, complete with its own airport and hotel complex. Australia's highly developed air transport system puts the whole continent within reach: beaches and ski resorts, dynamic cities and Outback towns.

A Laid-Back Culture

Even among such a wealth of natural wonders, it's the people you meet who often leave the deepest impression. Australians generally are a friendly, no-nonsense bunch – direct and to the point. 'Gidday mate!' is a cheery greeting often heard, sometimes followed by 'How ya goin', alright?' Americans detect Cockney or Irish overtones in the Australian accent – yet some visitors from Britain or Ireland swear they can identify an American influence.

Many Australian terms are unique, as likely to baffle a Brit or American as a European. 'Don't come the raw prawn' is a picturesque example, fading now from general usage. It means 'Don't try to pull the wool over my eyes.' The happy-go-lucky expression 'She'll be right' has been largely supplanted by 'No worries, mate,' but they both mean the same thing – 'It will all be OK.'

Sport is a big part of the Australian way of life

The Aussie sense of humour can bewilder newcomers. It is peppered with ironic understatements and playful contradictions, such as: 'She's getting a bit warm' (as the shade temperature reaches 40°C or 104°F); 'You're not wrong, mate' (an expression of enthusiastic agreement); or 'Now there's a bloke who hates a drink' (meaning that the man is a heavy drinker).

Another Aussie pastime

Australians have a love of outdoor enjoyment and a passion for sport, from the home-grown 'Aussie Rules' and old-established cricket to relatively new sports like baseball and basketball. The sunny climate has a lot to do with this, but so does the perception that the sporting field (or jogging track) is a place where social barriers are easily overcome.

Australia has a high proportion of migrants, and the nation's cultural mix is still evolving, but Britain and the US are still the main influences. British visitors often notice a California-style informality; American visitors are often surprised by the degree of Britishness remaining. At leisure, the majority of young Australians dress casually and watch American TV shows, but students at private schools continue to wear blazers and straw boaters like their counterparts in England. Cricket is played on local greens and lawyers appear in court in British-style gowns and horsehair wigs.

Of course, ethnic and other rivalries do exist. But underlying this cultural diversity is a fundamental tolerance, and a genuine desire for 'a fair go' – a wish for fairness in society, and, on the individual level, to be taken at face value and not judged on preconceptions of class, race or gender.

A BRIEF HISTORY

Australia may have been populated for longer than Western Europe – possibly twice as long. Experts are divided about the dates, with some scientists suggesting that the first inhabitants of Australia arrived from some location in Asia 50,000 or 60,000 years ago, others arguing that it was far earlier. Professor Paul Tacon, an eminent archaeologist at Griffith University, Queensland, claims that pollen core samples taken across Australia show changes in vegetation and deposition of charcoal 'beginning somewhere about 120,000 years ago'. He believes that these changes probably resulted from human activity.

The first migrations to Australia were most likely spurred by a period of glacial advance that encouraged the cave-dwellers of the Northern Hemisphere to head for the sun belt. This move set off a chain reaction, forcing more southerly folk out of their way. As ice caps accumulated, sea levels dropped drastically. So, in a search for greener pastures or more elbow-room, or perhaps blown off course, the original immigrants arrived Down Under by boat from the north.

The first Australians had little difficulty adapting to the new environment. As Stone Age hunter-gatherers, they were accustomed to foraging, and the takings in the new continent were good: plenty of fish, berries and roots and, for a change of diet, why not go out and spear a kangaroo?

'The Dreamtime' is the all-purpose name for everything that came before. It puts Aboriginal history, traditions and culture under a single mythological roof. The Dreamtime's version of Genesis recounts how ancestral heroes created the stars, the earth and all the creatures. The Dreamtime explains why the animals and plants are the way they are, and how humans can live in harmony with nature.

Aboriginal paintings reveal a developed aesthetic sense

Navigators Arrive

For many millennia the Aborigines had Australia to themselves. But over the last few hundred years, the rest of the world began closing in. Like the search for El Dorado, everybody seemed to be looking for *Terra Australis Incognita*, the 'Unknown Land of the South'. Throughout the 16th century, explorers from Europe kept their eyes peeled for the legendary continent and its presumed riches. Some (including the Spanish, Portuguese and Chinese) may have come close, but the first known landing was by a Dutch captain, Willem Jansz, in 1606. It was an anticlimax. 'There was no good to be done there,' was Jansz's conclusion as he weighed anchor.

The merchant adventurers of the Dutch East India Company were not to be discouraged, however. In 1642 the company dispatched one of its ace seafarers, Abel Tasman, to track down the elusive treasures of the farthest continent. On his first expedition, Tasman discovered an island that he called

Van Diemen's Land – now known as Tasmania, after him. A couple of years later he was sent back. He covered much of the coast of northern Australia, but still found no gold, silver or spices. Like Jansz before him, Tasman had nothing good to say about the indigenous people, who impressed him as poor, hungry and unattractive brutes. The Dutch named Australia New Holland, but their reports on the land were so unpromising that they never bothered to claim it.

Another pessimistic view was reported by a colourful traveller, English buccaneer William Dampier, who had two good looks at the west coast of Australia towards the end of the 17th century. He found no drinking water, no fruit or vegetables and no riches. The local inhabitants, he wrote, were 'the miserablest people in the world'.

Botany Bay

Almost by accident, Captain James Cook, the great British navigator, landed on the east coast of Australia in 1770 on a very roundabout trip back to England from Tahiti. Aboard his ship *Endeavour* were the skilled naturalists Joseph Banks and Daniel Solander. They found so many fascinating specimens that Cook was moved to name the place Botany Bay.

'Beautiful lies'

According to the author Mark Twain, the history of Australia 'does not read like history but like the most beautiful lies... It is full of surprises, and adventures, and incongruities, and contradictions, and incredibilities; but they are all true; they all happened.'

Cook claimed all the territory he charted for George III, coining the name New South Wales. He returned to London with glowing reports of the Australia he had seen: a vast, sunny, fertile land, inhabited by a native people who were 'far more happier than we Europeans'.

In 1779, Joseph Banks, by now president of the Royal

Society, came up with a novel idea. He proposed colonising Australia, but instead of conventional settlers, he would send out convicts as pioneers. This plan, he contended, would solve the crisis in Britain's overflowing jails.

For most of the 18th century, the British had disposed of troublesome convicts by banishing them to North America. With the American Revolution, though, this destination was no longer an option. The motherland's prisons could not cope, and the river hulks that were used as floating jails threatened riot and disease.

Cook's *Endeavour*, a converted collier, rides a storm

Banks's proposal for a prison island on the other side of the globe seemed far-fetched and expensive, but, with no alternatives, in May 1787 the British government began the transportation of criminals to Australia. The programme was to endure for 80 years. In that time more than 160,000 convicts were shipped to a new life Down Under.

The First Fleet

A retired naval officer, Captain Arthur Phillip, was put in command of the first fleet of 11 sailing vessels carrying nearly 1,500 people – more than half of them convicts – on an eight-month voyage from Portsmouth to New South Wales. Against the odds, the convoy was a success.

Captain Phillip (now with the title Governor) came ashore in full ceremonial dress but unarmed. Spear-toting Aborigines milled about like an unwelcoming committee. A lieutenant on the flagship wrote: 'I think it is very easy to conceive the ridiculous figure we must appear to these poor creatures, who were perfectly naked.' It also unveiled the truth about Botany Bay: Captain Cook's rosy claims faded to bleak. The expedition's officers were appalled to discover that there was no shelter from east winds, that much of the alleged meadowland was actually swamp and that there was not enough fresh water to go around.

Captain James Cook, as portrayed by Nathaniel Dance

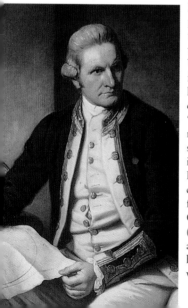

Luckily, the next best thing to paradise was waiting just around the corner. Governor Phillip and a reconnaissance party sailed 20km (12 miles) up the coast and discovered what Fleet Surgeon John White modestly called 'the finest and most extensive harbour in the universe'. It could, he determined provide 'safe anchorage for all the navies of Europe'. It was also strikingly beautiful. Today it is decorated with an Opera House and a bridge and is called Sydney Harbour. The fleet reassembled at Sydney Cove on 26 January 1788 (the date is marked every year as the Australian national holiday), and the British flag was raised over the colony.

London's great expectations took for granted that New South Wales would be instantly self-sufficient. Real life fell dangerously short of the theory. The Sydney summer was too hot for exertion, and even if the convicts had genuinely wanted to pitch in, the soil was unpromising. In any event, most of the outcasts were city-bred and didn't know the difference between a hoe and a sickle. Livestock died or disappeared in the bush.

Shipwrecks and delays in London meant that relief supplies were delayed for nearly two years of increasing desperation. As food supplies dwindled, rations were cut. Prisoners caught stealing food were flogged. Finally, to set an example, the Governor ordered a food looter to be hanged.

In June 1790, to all-round jubilation, the supply ship *Lady Juliana* reached Sydney harbour and the long fast ended. As agriculture finally began to blossom, many thousands of new prisoners were shipped out. And even voluntary settlers chose Australia as the land of their future.

Enter Captain Bligh

When Governor Phillip retired, the colony's top army officer, Major Francis Grose, took over. His army subordinates fared very well under the new regime, which encouraged free enterprise. The officers soon found profitable sidelines, usually at the expense of the British taxpayers. The army's monopoly on the sale of rum made quick fortunes; under some tipsy economic law, rum began to replace money as Australia's medium of exchange. Even prisoners were paid in alcohol for their extracurricular jobs.

As news of widespread hanky-panky reached London, the government responded by sending out a well-known disciplinarian to shake up the rum-sodden militia. He was Captain William Bligh, target of the notorious mutiny on HMS *Bounty* seven years earlier. Bligh meant to put fear into the hearts of backsliding officers, but his explosive temper was beyond control. His New South Wales victims nicknamed the new governor Caligula and plotted treason.

Bligh was deposed by a group of insurgent officers on 26 January 1808, as the colony toasted its 20th anniversary. The Rum Rebellion, as the mutiny was dubbed, led to a radical reorganisation and reshuffle in personnel. But the inevitable court-martial seemed to understand how Bligh's personality and methods had galled his subordinates. The mutineers were finally punished by more than a rap on the knuckles, but less than they might have expected.

Opening a Continent

New South Wales, under Governor Lachlan Macquarie, overcame the stigma of a penal colony and became a land of opportunity. The idealistic army officer organised the building of schools, a hospital and a courthouse, and roads to link them. As a method of inspiration for exiles to go straight

Brave but Fallible

Captain William Bligh would not have won any popularity contests, but historians believe that he was not as bad as is sometimes thought. Before his career in Australia, he had a distinguished record: he had circumnavigated the globe with Captain Cook, fought under Horatio Nelson at the Battle of Copenhagen, and shown evidence of a super-human survival instinct when the Bounty mutineers abandoned him in the Pacific. Thanks to his courage, his skill as a navigator, and good fortune, he survived a voyage of 5,823km (3,618 miles) in a lifeboat. By coincidence he had also been involved in another serious naval mutiny, in 1797, before being appointed Governor of New South Wales to re-establish discipline. This captain, immortalised by Hollywood, eventually reached the rank of Rear Admiral.

and win emancipation, Macquarie appointed an ex-convict as Justice of the Peace. Then he invited some of the others to dinner, much to the horror of the local élite. One of the criminals Macquarie pardoned, Francis Greenway, became the colony's prolific official architect.

Some of the ex-convicts fared so well under Macquarie's progressive policies that he was accused of pampering the criminal class.

Hyde Park Barracks, Sydney, designed by Francis Greenway

London ordered tougher punishment, and the separation of prisoners from the rest of the population. All this led to long-lasting conflict between reformed criminals and their children on one side and a privileged class of immigrants on the other. Nowadays, the shoe is on the other foot: descendants of First Fleet convicts often express the same kind of pride as Americans of *Mayflower* ancestry.

The biggest problem for Governor Macquarie and his immediate successors was the colony's position on the edge of the sea. There was not enough land to provide food for the expanding population. The Blue Mountains, which boxed in Sydney Cove, seemed a hopeless barrier. Every attempt to break through the labyrinth of steep valleys failed. Then, in 1813, explorers Blaxland, Wentworth and Lawson had the unconventional idea of crossing the peaks rather than the valleys. It worked. Beyond the Blue Mountains they discovered a land of plenty – endless plains that would support a great new society.

Other adventurers opened new territories. Land was either confiscated or bought from the indigenous tribesmen: for 400 sq km (150 sq miles) of what is now Melbourne, the

The Prospector dreams of riches in an 1889 painting

entrepreneurs gave the Aborigines a wagonload of clothing and blankets plus 30 knives, 12 tomahawks, 10 mirrors, 12 pairs of scissors and 23kg (50lb) of flour. By the middle of the 19th century, thousands of settlers had poured into Australia and all of the present state capitals were on the map.

Age of Gold

In his understandable enthusiasm, prospector Edward Hargraves slightly overstated the case when he declared: 'This is a memorable day in the history of New South Wales. I shall be a baronet.' The year was 1851. The place was near Bathurst, approximately 210km (130 miles) west of Sydney. Hargraves' audience consisted of one speechless colleague. The occasion was the discovery of gold in Australia.

No sooner had the news of the Bathurst find reached the farthest corner of the land than prospectors from Melbourne struck gold at Ballarat. With two colonies – New South Wales and Victoria – sharing in the boom, adventurers streamed in from both Europe and America. By the year 1860 Australia's population had reached a total of one million. Thirty-three years later the bonanza became a coast-to-coast celebration when gold was discovered in Kalgoorlie in Western Australia.

Life in the gold fields was rugged, aggravated by climate, flies and tax collectors. Whether big winners or, more likely, small losers, all the diggers had to pay the same licence fee. Enforcement and fines were needlessly strict. Justice, the miners felt, was tilted against them. So they burned their licences and demonstrated for voting rights and other reforms. In the subsequent siege of the Eureka Stockade in Ballarat in 1854, troops were ordered to attack the demonstrators. There was heavy loss of life, and the licence fee was abandoned.

Another riot, in 1861, pitted the white prospectors against Chinese miners, who were resented for their foreignness, strong work ethic and frugality. At Lambing Flat, New South Wales, thousands of whites whipped and clubbed a community of Chinese. Police, troops and finally the courts were lenient on the attackers. It was the worst of several race riots. With the tensions of the gold rush, the notion of the 'yellow peril' was embedded in Australia's national consciousness.

Rogues on the Range

Transportation of convicts finally ended in 1868, when London had to admit that the threat of exile in Australia was no deterrent to crime. In Australia itself, crime was always something of a problem; nobody really expected every last sinner to go straight as soon as he arrived. Several wily characters, often escaped convicts, became bushrangers, the local version of highwaymen. They occasionally attracted sympathy from Outback folk because they tended to rob the rich and flout authority. As the crimes grew more ambitious or outrageous, their fame was frozen into legend.

The saga of Ned Kelly (1854–80) reads like Robin Hood gone sour. The Kelly gang preyed on bankers rather than humble farmers, and Kelly's imaginative operations could be spectacular. But he killed more than his fair share of policemen, almost for the fun of it. Wounded in a shootout, Kelly tried to escape in a suit of homemade armour; this nightmarish contraption deflected most of the bullets, and he was captured wounded but alive. Sentenced to death, he cheekily invited the judge to meet him in the hereafter. Only two weeks after Kelly was hanged, the judge, indeed, died.

Melbourne's shrine to the dead of World War I

An Independent Nation

Having received the blessing of Queen Victoria, the colonies of Australia formed a new nation, the Commonwealth of Australia, on New Year's Day 1901. This federation retained the Queen as head of state, and also bowed to the parliament and Privy Council in London.

Loyalty to the British Empire was tested twice, extravagantly, in the world wars. The Allied defeat at Gallipoli in 1915 was the first and most memorable single disaster for the Australian troops. By the end of World War I, over 200,000 Australians – two-thirds of the expeditionary force – had been killed or wounded.

Combat came closer to home in World War II, when Japanese planes repeatedly bombed Darwin, enemy submarines penetrated Sydney harbour and sank a ferry (the torpedo had been fired at the American warship USS *Chicago*), ships were sunk off the Australian coast and a couple of shells hit Sydney's eastern suburbs. American forces under General MacArthur arrived in Australia in 1942 and a US force supported by Australia defeated the Japanese decisively in the Battle of the Coral Sea in May of that year. The statistics: 27,000 Australian servicemen died in action on the European and Asian fronts, and nearly 8,000 more died as prisoners of Japan. Almost one in three Australians taken prisoner by the Japanese died in captivity.

Anzac Day remembers Australia's fallen soldiers

After the war, Britain aligned itself with Europe and downgraded its ties with the old Empire. As Britain's regional power declined, Australia boosted its alliance with the US. Australian troops (more than 40,000 of them) fought alongside Americans in Vietnam, sparking vehement anti-war protests in Sydney and other Australian cities. Australian Prime Minister Harold Holt introduced the draft and promised US President Lyndon B. Johnson that Australia would go 'all the way with LBJ'. Holt disappeared in 1967 while swimming at Cheviot Beach south of Melbourne; it is believed he was caught in the undertow and swept out to sea.

The tilt towards the US and Asia also showed up in Australia's balance of trade. Prior to World War II, 42 percent of Australia's overseas trade was with Britain. Today, Australia's

Greek city?

Thanks to its immigrant population, Melbourne is often called the third greatest Greek city, after Athens and Thessaloniki.

top 10 export markets include Japan, Singapore, China, Korea, Taiwan, India and Thailand. Japan buys almost one fifth of Australia's total merchandise exports. Among non-Asian markets, the most significant for Australian exporters are the US, New Zealand and Britain.

Cultural Changes

Another obvious change in orientation is the racial and national background of Australians. Before World War II, 98 percent of the population was of British or Irish birth or descent. As for immigrants, 81 percent of Australia's overseas-born population came from the main English-speaking countries (Britain, Ireland, New Zealand, South Africa, Canada and the USA). Since then, the fortress walls of the infamous 'White Australia' immigration policy (enacted in 1901 to maintain racial purity) have been torn down under the slogan 'Populate or Perish.' Australia has seen immigration from many countries including Italy, Greece, Malta, the former Yugoslavia, Vietnam, Germany, the Netherlands, the Philippines, Malaysia, Lebanon, Turkey, Hong Kong, China, South Africa, Sudan, Afghanistan and Iraq.

Since 1945, Australia has accepted 6.5 million people as new settlers – about 660,000 of whom arrived under humanitarian programmes – creating a culturally diverse nation. Nearly a quarter of Australia's population is overseas-born. By 2006, only 34 percent of the overseas-born population had been born in English-speaking countries.

Australia has had a less than comfortable relationship with its own indigenous peoples, the Aborigines and Torres Strait Islanders. Together, they make up just over 2 percent of the population (about 90 per cent are Aborigines). Aborigines were not permitted to vote in national elections until 1962, and were not included in the census until 1967. Worse, from the late 19th century until about 1970, governments forcibly removed as many as 100,000 Aboriginal children, mainly of mixed race, from their families. The children – later dubbed the Stolen Generations – were taken to church missions, orphanages and foster homes.

In 1990, a government commission gave indigenous peoples the power to make decisions on social and other matters that affect them. In 1993, there were further moves towards reconciliation, with legislation effectively nullifying the doctrine of *terra nullius* ('uninhabited land'), which had deemed Australia to be empty at the time of European settlement and, by default, the property of the Crown. The court ruling recognised that Aborigines may hold common law rights or 'native title' to land.

Traditional Aboriginal art depicts the Dreamtime

Support continues to grow for a treaty with the Aboriginal people to foster national unity. In 2000, in cities throughout Australia, many thousands of citizens marched to demand that the government formally apologise to the Stolen Generations, to begin a process of reconciliation. In Sydney,

250,000 people marched for the cause. However, no progress on the issue was made until February 2008, when Labor prime minister Kevin Rudd issued an apology. It remains to be seen what further steps will be taken.

Republican Leanings

In the 1990s, Labor prime minister Paul Keating argued that Australia should become a republic, and engage strongly with Asia. His Liberal Party successor, John Howard, who won the 1996 election, was cut from very different political cloth. Under his stewardship Australia looked less towards Asia and more to traditional alliances with Europe and the US. In a 1999 referendum, a prototype republic was put to the vote – and rejected. Opinion polls show that Australians do, in fact, favour a republic, but they disliked the model put forward, which proposed that politicians, rather than the people, should elect the president. So Australia still has Britain's monarch as its head of state (represented here by a governor-general), and the Union Jack adorning its flag. The new Labor prime minister, Kevin Rudd, has promised to hold another referendum on the issue.

The Union flag still occupies a quarter of the Australian flag

Australia entered the 21st century in an up-beat mood and with a booming economy, but the nation's ability to stand up to the new century's challenges is still in question. Australia's economy proved more vulnerable to the global financial crisis than was expected, and scientists predict that climate change will affect the country severely in coming years, causing more severe droughts and bush fires.

Historical Landmarks

50,000BC The Aborigines arrive on the Australian continent.

1606 Willem Jansz is the first European to land.

1642 Abel Tasman discovers Tasmania and New Zealand.

1770 Captain James Cook explores the east coast of Australia, which he calls New South Wales.

1788 Britain establishes a penal colony in Sydney Cove.

1808 The 'Rum Rebellion' overthrows Captain William Bligh.

1851 Gold is discovered in New South Wales.

1854 Battle of the Eureka Stockade, Ballarat.

1901 Six colonies federated into the Commonwealth of Australia.

1914–18 330,000 Australians serve in World War I; 60,000 are killed, 165,000 wounded.

1917 Opening of the transcontinental railway.

1927 Federal parliament moves from Melbourne to Canberra.

1928 Royal Flying Doctor Service founded in Queensland.

1939–45 World War II: Australian Air Force active in Britain; navy operates in Mediterranean; soldiers fight in North Africa and the Pacific.

1956 Olympic Games held in Melbourne. First Australian TV.

1960 Australia grants citizenship to Aborigines.

1962 Aborigines allowed to vote in federal elections.

1972 'White Australia' immigration policy is abandoned.

1973 Sydney Opera House is finally completed.

1985 Uluru (Ayers Rock), Kata Tjuta (The Olgas) and surrounding desert are returned to Aboriginal owners.

1993 The Aborigines' right to own land is recognised.

1999 Referendum rejects prototype republic.

2000 Olympic Games in Sydney.

2001 Australia celebrates the centenary of Federation.

2003 Australian government supports US military action in Iraq.

2007 Labor Party elected to power

2008 Prime Minister Rudd apologises to the Stolen Generations.

2009 173 people killed by devastating bush fires in Victoria.

WHERE TO GO

Deciding where to go and what to see in Australia may be the hardest part of the journey. How can you squeeze so much into a limited time? Where to go in such a vast country?

About 36 million passengers a year fly Australia's domestic airline routes. Budget airlines make flying from city to city an affordable option, although it's best to plan ahead to get the best fares and flight times. Alternatives are slower, but often more revealing: try the transcontinental trains and the long-distance buses, some equipped for luxury travel.

Since you probably can't see all of it, you'll have to arrange your tour of Australia to concentrate on seeing a manageable slice or two of the continent. Planning your itinerary requires a compromise involving the time and funds you have available, the season, your special interests and your choice of gateway city. Sydney is the main gateway into Australia, but some airlines allow you to arrive in Cairns, for example, and depart from Sydney or Perth.

This section of the guide is arranged according to the geographic reality of Australia's states. Although there is no visible difference between the red deserts of the Northern Territory and those of South Australia, it's convenient to consider them in the context of the political frontiers. Besides, the way that history and chance carved Australia into states comes close to providing a fairly natural division into sightseeing regions.

In each state or territory we start with the capital city gateway and fan out from there. We begin where Australia itself began, at Sydney Cove. After a side trip to the federal capital, Canberra, we continue beyond New South Wales, in an anticlockwise circuit from Queensland to Victoria, ending with a look at the continent's lovely green footnote, Tasmania.

Sydney, with the famous Opera House in the foreground

NEW SOUTH WALES

Sydney can't help but dominate New South Wales (NSW), if only because most of the state's population lives in the capital. However, beyond the metropolis, the state – six times the size of England – is as varied as dairyland and desert or vineyards and craggy mountains.

Sydney

Sydney is Australia's oldest, liveliest and biggest city (total population 4.3 million). If the world had a lifestyle capital, Sydney would be a strong contender – something that is richly ironic, considering that the city started out as a British penal colony. Sydney is sun-drenched, brawny, energetic, fun-loving and outdoor-oriented. It ranks highly in world lists of favourite tourist destinations; its residents know this and they revel in it. After hours – and Sydneysiders do live

for the after hours – Sydney offers every imaginable cosmopolitan delight. It's a sunny coincidence that beaches famous for surfing and scenery are only minutes away.

Most of the world's great cities have a famous landmark that serves as an instantly recognisable symbol. Sydney has two: the perfect steel arch of Sydney Harbour Bridge and the billowing shell-like roofs of the Sydney Opera House. That's what happens when engineers and architects embellish a harbour coveted by artists as well as admirals.

Sydney Harbour has been stealing the show ever since the first convicts arrived in 1788 to start a new nation. For a quick appreciation of the intricacies of **Port Jackson** (the

The Opera House and the Sydney Harbour Bridge

official name for Sydney Harbour), gaze out from the top of Sydney Tower, Sydney's tallest building. See the clear blue tentacles of water stretching from the South Pacific into the heart of the city. Schools of sailing boats vaunt the harbour's perfection in the reflection of the skyscrapers, the classic Sydney Harbour Bridge and the exhilarating opera house. It's a pity that Captain Cook never noticed this glorious setting as he sailed right past on his way home to England from Botany Bay. Sydney Harbour National Park fringes a long, leafy stretch of the northern side of the harbour and also includes some harbour islands and a chunk of the southern foreshore. For information about harbour sights, *see page 56*.

Exploring Sydney Harbour is as easy as jumping on a commuter ferry or taking a sightseeing tour. Most tours – by land or sea – leave from **Circular Quay** (short for Semi-Circular Quay, as it was more accurately named in olden times). Although cruise ships and water taxis alike dock here, most of the action involves ferries, which sail to various destinations including the zoo *(see page 57)*, and 'Jetcat' catamarans, the fastest way to reach seaside Manly *(see page 58)*. The quay's quota of human interest features hasty travellers, leisurely sightseers, street musicians, artists, hawkers and people

Circular Quay, the terminus for Sydney's many ferries

just 'hanging out'. Whether you see Australia's busiest harbour from the deck of a luxury liner, a sightseeing boat, or a humble ferry, don't miss this invigorating angle on the city's skyline.

The Rocks

To start at the beginning, stroll through the charming streets of **The Rocks** – just west of Circular Quay – the neighbourhood where Sydney was born. You can take a 90-minute guided walking tour (to book, tel: (02) 9247 6678) or conduct your own tour. Here modern Australia's founding fathers – convicts who had been charged with anything from shoplifting to major forgery – came ashore in 1788 to build the colony of New South Wales. This historic waterfront district has everything a tourist could want: lovely views at long and short range, moody old buildings, cheerful plazas and plenty of distractions in the way of shopping, eating and drinking. There are plenty of tourists too!

But it nearly was not so. The Rocks was once one of Sydney's most squalid and dangerous quarters, a Dickensian warren of warehouses, grog shops and brothels, where the rum was laced with tobacco juice and the larrikin 'razor gangs' preyed on the unwary. An outbreak of bubonic plague in 1900 was a low-light in The Rocks' sordid history.

The whole area was due to be levelled for redevelopment in the 1970s, but there was fierce resistance from residents and academics, and the project was thwarted when the construction unions, led by activist Jack Mundey, refused to start work. This was the beginning of the Green movement to preserve whatever was atmospheric about Old Sydney.

A wide range of local leaflets and maps is on offer at the **Sydney Visitor Centre** (open daily 9.30am–5.30pm; <www.sydneyvisitorcentre.com>; cnr Argyle and Playfair streets). You can book tours there as well.

Cadman's Cottage, nearby, is central Sydney's oldest (1816) surviving house – a simple stone cottage occupied for many years by the government's official boatsman. It's now the information centre for Sydney Harbour National Park. Not far away, the **Museum of Contemporary Art** (open daily 10am–5pm; <www.mca.com.au>; free) gives new life to an Art Deco building. The museum's collection ranges from Aboriginal bark paintings to the latest – and strangest – installation works. There are also plenty of touring exhibitions. The café on the terrace (with harbour view) is excellent.

Just south of The Rocks, on Bridge Street, the fascinating **Museum of Sydney** (open daily 9.30am–5pm; admission fee) on the site of the first Government House, promises to take visitors on 'a journey of discovery' from 1788 to the present day.

North of Cadman's Cottage are solid 19th-century bond stores, now converted to offices and shops such as **Campbells Storehouse** (eating, souvenirs, arts and

Outside the Museum of Sydney

Street performance

crafts). Heading west from Cadman's Cottage you'll arrive at the similar **Argyle Stores**. Beyond is the **Argyle Cut**, a massive excavation hacked out with pickaxes through sandstone cliffs by convict labour-gangs. At the top of Argyle Cut, Cumberland Street provides access to Sydney Harbour Bridge via **Cumberland Steps**. In Cumberland Street not far away, the **Australian Hotel**, a friendly pub in the older Aussie tradition, stocks beers from every state in the country. It is one of only two pubs in Sydney to serve Bavarian-style unfiltered beers created by master brewer Geoff Scharer, acclaimed as the best in Australia.

A little further on, in Argyle Place, you will find a neat row of terraced houses straight out of Georgian England. Two other old pubs in this area deserve mention. The quaint **Hero of Waterloo** at 81 Lower Fort Street was built in 1843 on top of a maze of subterranean cellars through which drunken patrons were conveyed to be sold as crew to unscrupulous sea captains. That practice has died out but the cellars remain.

The **Lord Nelson Brewery Hotel**, a square sandstone block of a building at the corner of Kent and Argyle Street, was built c1840 and has maintained something of a British naval atmosphere ever since. It brews its own beers, some of them pretty potent.

For history without the refreshments, visit the sandstone Garrison Church, officially named the **Holy Trinity Anglican Church**, which dates from the early 1840s. As the unofficial name indicates, it was the church for members of the garrison regiment, the men in charge of the convict colony. It's now a fashionable place to get married.

At the start of George Street, close to the Irish-influenced Mercantile Hotel, **The Rocks Market** (Sat–Sun 10am–5pm) takes place every weekend under a 150-m (492-ft) long canopy. Street entertainers perform, while stall-holders sell crafts, souvenirs, toys and gifts. Not far away, Customs Officers Stairs lead down to some charming harbourside restaurants housed in old bond stores, fronting **Campbells Cove**. Just across the harbour is the Opera House.

Overhanging The Rocks, **Observatory Hill** is a perfect place from which to gaze at the sky or at Sydney Harbour. This is the highest point of the city, visible for kilometres around. Since the middle of the 19th century, at 1pm precisely every day, a ball is dropped from the top of a mast to enable sea captains to check their chronometers. **Sydney Observatory** (open daily 10am–5pm; <www. sydneyobservatory.com.au>) is now a museum of astronomy, and opens every evening (times vary according to season) for talks, films and stargazing (bookings, tel: (02) 9217 0485).

Another favourite lookout is **Dawes Point Park**, with its scattering of old cannons, from where you can watch the ferries and sailing boats.

Campbells Cove, The Rocks

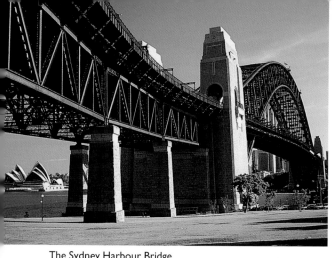

The Sydney Harbour Bridge

➤ Here, you're in the shadow of the **Sydney Harbour Bridge**, with its drive-through stone pylons (purely ornamental) and colossal steel arch. The bridge stars on television each New Year's Eve, when it serves as a platform for a spectacular fireworks display. To bid farewell to the old year and welcome in the new, fireworks are fired from the arch in a spectacular display. Other fireworks on the road-span create a Niagara-like cascade into Sydney Harbour.

Linking the city and the north, the bridge's single arch is 503m (1,650ft) across, and wide enough to carry eight lanes of cars and two railway tracks, as well as lanes for pedestrians and cyclists. When it was built, during the Great Depression, Sydneysiders called the bridge the Iron Lung, because it kept a lot of people 'breathing' – by giving them jobs. It takes 10 years to repaint the steel-grey bridge, at the end of which it's time to start again. To ease traffic congestion a tunnel has also been built under the harbour.

An unusual vantage point for viewing the bridge, the harbour and the harbour and the skyline is from the top of one of the bridge's massive pylons. The **Pylon Lookout** (open daily 10am–5pm; <www.pylonlookout.com.au>; admission fee) is in the southeast tower, which also contains a museum; the stairway can be reached via Cumberland Street, The Rocks.

A company called BridgeClimb (tel: (02) 8274 7777; <www.bridgeclimb.com.au>) conducts guided walks for small groups over the bridge's massive arches. Not across the walkway below, but over the arches above. For decades, groups of daredevils had been doing this illicitly. Since the legal climb began in 1998 the waiting list has grown quite long and it pays to book your climb as far in advance as you can. You can even do the climb at dawn, twilight or at night, though excursions are understandably postponed during electrical storms. It's not a cheap thrill: tickets start from A$179, and cost more for twilight or dawn climbs or at weekends (minimum age 12).

City Centre

A similar tour operates from the top of **Sydney Tower** at Centrepoint (corner of Pitt and Market streets; open daily 9am–10.30pm, till 11.30pm Sat), the city's highest vantage point, at 305m (1,001ft) above the street. Skywalk (tel: (02) 9222 9491; <www.skywalk.com.au>) offers walks outside the tower's turret but, for those without a head for heights, it takes only 40 seconds to reach the observation decks, where amateur photographers get that

Pipped at the post

In 1932, at the opening ceremony of the Harbour Bridge, the leader of a fanatical right-wing group, Francis Edward de Groot, rode up on a horse and sliced through the ribbon with a sword before the left-wing premier of NSW, Jack Lang, could cut it.

glazed look as they peer through the tinted windows to unlimited horizons. On a flawless day you can see all the way north to Terrigal and south to Wollongong, far out to sea to the east, or as far west as the Blue Mountains. Otherwise, look down at the seething shopping streets around the tower. Pedestrians-only **Pitt Street Mall** is one of the city's main retail centres, home to department stores and shops of all kinds. The **Strand Arcade**, which runs off the Mall, is a grand old shopping arcade full of up-market boutiques.

A short distance towards the harbour is the city's main square, **Martin Place**, flanked by the imposing Victorian **General Post Office** (GPO) building. This has been imaginatively converted into a stylish modern complex including a five-star hotel.

The Sydney Tower has great views from the top

From the same era, but even grander, the sandstone **Queen Victoria Building** (open Mon–Sat 9am–6pm, Thur 9am–9pm, Sun 11am–5pm; <www.qvb.com.au>) occupies a whole block on George Street opposite the Town Hall. The Byzantine-style 'QVB' began as a municipal market and commercial centre, including a hotel and a concert hall, topped by statuary and some 21 domes.

Built in 1898 to commemorate Queen Victoria's Golden Jubilee, it was faithfully restored in the 1980s to create a magnificent all-weather shopping centre housing nearly 200 chic boutiques, cafés and restaurants, in a cool and unhurried atmosphere of period charm. Pierre Cardin called it 'the most beautiful shopping centre in the world'. There are more shopping opportunities across George Street at the much more recently built **Galeries Victoria**.

Stained glass at the QVB

Next door to the QVB, Sydney's **Town Hall** (open daily 9am–5pm) enlivens a site that used to be a cemetery. The Victorian building, home of the city council, is also used for concerts and exhibitions. The Anglican **St Andrew's Cathedral** next to it dates from 1868.

Chinatown and Darling Harbour

After dark, young Sydneysiders flock to the section of George Street heading south from the Town Hall, lined with video entertainment arcades, fast-food joints and a cinema complex. Sydney's fledgling Spanish Quarter begins nearby on the corner of George Street and Liverpool Street – there's a choice of tapas bars here.

In the adjacent Chinatown district, gourmets can enjoy the delights of Peking, Cantonese and Szechuan cuisine. The substantial local Chinese community is joined by Sydneysiders and tourists enjoying the Chinese cafés, restaurants and shops selling exotic spices and knick-knacks. The district's centrepiece is **Dixon Street**, a pedestrian zone framed by ceremonial gates.

If you're in the area at the right time, check out **Paddy's Market** in Hay Street (open Thur–Sun 9am–5pm), a brick building beneath a skyscraper called Market City. Paddy's is full of stalls selling almost anything from seashells and sunglasses to fruit and vegetables. Market City has plenty of Chinese and other Asian eateries to satisfy hunger pangs.

Nearby, the modern leisure precinct of **Darling Harbour** is well stocked with shops, restaurants and attractions, and a **monorail** and light rail system link it to more central areas. On the city side of Darling Harbour lie **Cockle Bay** and its extension, **King Street Wharf**, complexes of bars and restaurants. These areas have proved much more popular than the shopping and dining complex overlooking the harbour on the western side, mainly because they are easier to reach on foot from downtown Sydney.

Not far away, **Sydney Aquarium** (open daily 9am–10pm; <www.sydneyaquarium.com.au>; admission fee) is one of the largest in the world. In its Open Ocean Oceanarium, large sharks weigh up to 300kg (660lb) and measure over 9m (30ft) long. The Great Barrier Reef Complex houses over 6,000 creatures, and a visit there is the closest thing to diving on the reef without getting wet. The adjacent **Sydney Wildlife World** (open daily 9am–10pm; <www.sydneywildlifeworld.com.au>; admission fee) is a mini-zoo showcasing a selection of native fauna, from lizards and snakes to parrots and wallabies. The star attractions, however, are the koalas, which, for an extra fee, you can have your photo taken with.

Kids love Sydney Aquarium

The monorail links Darling Harbour to downtown Sydney

Other nearby attractions include the **National Maritime Museum** (open daily 9.30am–5pm, till 6pm in Jan; <www.anmm.gov.au>; free), a Chinese garden (open daily 9.30am–5pm), an IMAX cinema, and the **Sydney Entertainment Centre**, which is used for concerts. Beyond the Maritime Museum, in Pyrmont, is **Star City Casino** (open daily 24 hours).

Parks and Gardens

Although Sydney's lush **Hyde Park** is only a fraction the size of its namesake in London, it still provides the same sort of green relief. Like most big-city parks, however, it should be avoided after sunset. The most formal feature of the semi-formal gardens, the **Anzac War Memorial**, commemorates the World War I fighters in monumental art deco style, with later acknowledgments to the World War II contingent.

Sightseers interested in old churches should mark a few targets on the edge of Hyde Park. To the north, the early

Tropical plants in the Royal Botanic Gardens

colonial **St James's Church** in Queens Square was the work of the convict architect Francis Greenway. Just across College Street on the east is the Catholic **St Mary's Cathedral**.

You can view the cathedral's spires while immersed in a swimming pool next door at **Cook and Phillip Park** (open Mon–Fri 6am–10pm, Sat–Sun and public holidays 7am–8pm), an aquatic, fitness and recreation centre. You can't readily see the complex from the street, yet when you're inside its huge windows give views and let in lots of light. There are three pools – one with a wave machine. There's a café inside, or, if you want to eat alfresco, Bodhi's vegan restaurant does good business just outside.

The ornate **Great Synagogue** (tours Tues and Thur at noon) faces the park across Elizabeth Street. Jews have lived in Sydney since the arrival of the first shipment of prisoners.

The **Australian Museum** (open daily 9.30am–5pm; tel: (02) 9320 6000; <www.austmus.gov.au>; admission fee) on

College Street specialises in natural history and anthropology. Highlights include a dinosaur gallery (complete with models of giant-sized marsupials), a hands-on plant and animal identification centre, a gallery devoted to Australia's unique ecosystems, the Indigenous Australians exhibition, and a human evolution gallery. The museum is in the middle of a major renovation programme, and some galleries will be closed; check with the museum before visiting.

Hyde Park Barracks, (open daily 9.30am– 5pm; admission fee), designed by Greenway, located between Hyde Park and the Botanic Gardens, is now a museum of social history. On the top floor, one large room is a reconstruction of the dormitory life of the prisoners who once slept there. The **Mint**, next door, processed gold-rush bullion in the mid-19th century.

Another large park adjacent to Hyde Park is called the **Domain**, where concerts are held in summer. On one side of the Domain is the **Art Gallery of New South Wales** (open daily 10am–5pm; <www.artgallery.nsw.gov.au>; free), which consists of a formal exterior decorated with much bronze statuary and a modern extension, which infuses light into the building and provides sweeping views of east Sydney, part of the harbour, and the suburb of Woolloomooloo. An afternoon at the Art Gallery will give you a crash course in more than a century of traditional and modern Australian art. The **Yiribana Gallery** there is devoted to Aboriginal art and Torres Islander art (free guided tours Tues–Sun at 11am).

Sydney's **Royal Botanic Gardens** (open daily 7am– sunset; free guided walks daily at 10.30am) began as a different sort of garden: here the early colonists tried – with very limited success – to grow vegetables. Only a few steps from the busy skyscraper world of downtown Sydney, you can relax in the shade of Moreton Bay fig trees, palms or mahoganies, or enter the Tropical Centre (open daily 10am–4pm; admission fee), two glass pyramids full of orchids and other tropical beauties. Near the Tropical Centre, overlooking the duck pond, is a café-restaurant where you can relax in the peaceful surroundings.

There are several entrances to the Gardens and many paths; the most popular entrance is by the Opera House. From here the gardens curve down around Farm Cove to a peninsula called **Mrs Macquarie's Point**. The lady thus immortalised, the wife of the go-ahead governor, used to admire the view from here. Nearby is the venue for the summer season of outdoor films which are shown here during the Sydney Festival. There's a lot to see in the Gardens, and if you're feeling tired, you can take advantage of the hop-on hop-off Trackless Train, which does a 20-minute loop between the Opera House Gate and the Woolloomooloo Gate near the Art Gallery.

Centennial Park, most easily reached from the eastern end of Oxford Street in the inner-city suburb of **Paddington**, has provided greenery and fresh air to city folk since 1888, when it was dedicated on the centenary of Australia's foundation to 'the enjoyment of the people of New South Wales forever'. The park's 220 hectares (544 acres) of trees, lawns, duck ponds, rose gardens and bridle-paths are visited by about three million people a year, who cycle, roller-blade, walk their dogs, feed birds, play team sports, throw frisbees, fly kites, picnic and barbecue seafood or sausages.

If you fancy a ride on the bridle path, horse rental can be arranged from Moore Park Stables (tel: (02) 9360 8747). Bicycles and pedal-carts can be hired from Centennial Park Cycles (tel: (02) 9398 5027). **Centennial Park Kiosk** is a lovely setting for a meal and a glass of wine. Beside it stands a charming, if curious, modern stone fountain.

The **Belvedere Amphitheatre** here provides an outdoor venue for events and productions. In summer, a popular Moonlight Cinema programme is held there. Films start at about 8.30pm, and tickets are available at the gate from 7pm (or by phoning 1300 551 908; <www.moonlight.com.au>).

The cream 'sails' of the Opera House gleam in the sun

Sydney Opera House

There's a real sense of occasion and style about the structure of the **Sydney Opera House** (guided one-hour tours daily, every half-hour 9am–5pm; <www.sydneyoperahouse.com>), both inside and out. This unique building, covered in a million tiles, has achieved the seemingly impossible by improving a virtually perfect harbour. Yet its controversial architect left the country in a huff at an early stage of construction.

Until the arrival of the opera house, the promontory was the location of a tram depot, and in the 1950s the government of New South Wales decided to build a performing arts centre on the site. In 1957, a Danish architect, Jørn Utzon, won an international competition to design the building, and his novel plan included problems of spherical geometry so tricky that he actually chopped up a wooden sphere to prove it could be done. The shell of the complex was almost complete when Utzon walked out in 1966 due to pressure from the state government; the interior, which was in dispute, became the work of a committee. Despite this, from the tip of its highest roof (67m/220ft above sea level) to the Drama Theatre's orchestra pit (more than a fathom below sea level), this place has grace, taste and class. (Utzon has never returned to Sydney, but he accepted a role as advisor for any renovations.)

The name 'Sydney Opera House' is as renowned world-wide as it is inaccurate. The actual opera theatre is only one of the centre's five, and it is not the biggest.

Kings Cross and Paddington

East of the Domain is the district of **Woolloomooloo** (the name has something to do with kangaroos in an Aboriginal language). A spelling teaser for Australian school children, Woolloomooloo was threatened by demolition in the 1970s, but was saved by resident protests and union 'green bans'.

East of Woolloomooloo, bright lights and shady characters exist side by side in Kings Cross, one railway stop from Martin Place. 'The Cross', as it's often called, is Sydney's version of Pigalle, in Paris, or London's Soho – neon-filled, a bit tacky but rather fun, crawling with hedonists of all persuasions. Action continues 24 hours a day, with a diverting cavalcade of humanity – the brightly coloured, the bizarre, the stoned, the happy and the drunk. On weekends, tourists flock to the Cross to glimpse a bit of weirdness. Sometimes though, the weirdest characters they spot are other tourists.

The Cross's 'main drag' (major street) is **Darlinghurst Road**, bohemian verging on sleazy and dotted with strip joints, fast-food outlets, tattoo parlours and X-rated book and video shops, backpacker hostels and cheap hotels. Gentrification is progressing rapidly, however, and several stylish bars, restaurants and hotels have recently opened. The neighbouring area of Potts Point offers good eating – try Fratelli Paradiso just off Macleay Street.

A five-minute walk from Kings Cross Station brings you to **Elizabeth Bay House** (open Tues–Sun 10am–4.30pm), a superb example of colonial architecture, built in 1835 – and a reminder that this locality was once highly respectable.

If you have time for one more inner suburb, make it **Paddington**, to the southeast of Kings Cross. Its trademark is the intricate wrought-ironwork, known as Sydney Lace, on the balconies of 19th-century terraced houses. This feature, and the rather bohemian atmosphere, reminds some travellers of New Orleans. After decades of dilapidation, the district came up in the world rapidly as a fashionable, rather artsy place to live. It has developed into one of Sydney's most sought-after suburbs, with house prices to match. 'Paddo', as the locals call it, offers plenty of good restaurants, antiques shops, art galleries, good bookshops and trendy boutiques. One of the best markets in Sydney, **Paddington Markets**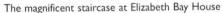

The magnificent staircase at Elizabeth Bay House

Paddington ironwork

(Sat 10am–4pm) is held in the grounds of Paddington Uniting Church, 395 Oxford Street. It offers almost every type of art and craft and is enlivened by a variety of street entertainers.

Paddington's main street, **Oxford Street**, which continues into the neighbouring suburb of **Darlinghurst**, is one of the hubs of Sydney's large gay community (others include Surry Hills, Newtown and Erskineville). The **Sydney Gay and Lesbian Mardi Gras** parade, held here in late February/early March, has become a respected institution. The street is home to two good bookshops, Ariel and Berkelouw, and three of its more imaginative cinemas, the Chauvel, the Verona and the Palace Academy Twin. **Victoria Barracks** is Oxford Street's renowned example of mid-19th-century military architecture, built by convicts to house a regiment of British soldiers and their families.

Around Sydney Harbour

Take a harbour cruise to appreciate hidden beaches, islets, mansions old and new, and even a couple of unsung bridges. Various companies run half-day and full-day excursions, or you can hop aboard a commuter ferry and get off where you like. You could also rent a boat of your own in which to weave around the rest of the nautical traffic.

Fort Denison, situated on a small island, is graphically nicknamed 'Pinchgut'. Before the construction of a proper prison, the colony's more troublesome convicts were banished to the rock to subsist on a bread-and-water diet. In the middle of the 19th century the island was fortified to guard Sydney from the far-fetched threat of a Russian military strike. Ironically, the only attack came in World War II when an American warship, conducting target practice, hit old Pinchgut by mistake. You can visit Fort Denison, but only as part of a guided tour conducted by a national parks ranger (to book, tel: (02) 9247 5033).

Taronga Zoo (open daily 9am–5pm; <www.zoo.nsw. gov.au>; admission fee), a 12-minute ferry ride from Circular Quay, has an excellent collection of native and non-native animals in a superb setting. Over the heads of the giraffes you can see across the harbour to the skyscrapers of Sydney. The zoo's Nocturnal House features indigenous night-time creatures illuminated in artificial moonlight, unaware of onlookers. The Rainforest Aviary houses hundreds of tropical birds. If you arrange your visit around feeding times, you can watch the keepers distribute food while they give talks about their charges.

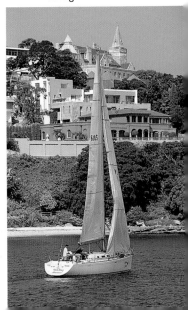

Sailing on the harbour

The ferry that goes to Taronga Zoo also stops at **Cremorne Point**, where there are excellent views of the city and harbour. A paved path winds from here along the shore of Mosman Bay to the Mosman ferry wharf, a distance that can be covered easily in about 90 minutes. You can then catch a ferry back to Circular Quay from Mosman.

Another popular ferry destination is **Watsons Bay**, in the Eastern Suburbs. This suburb began as a small fishing community and it still retains a village-like atmosphere. Doyle's on the Beach seafood restaurant is located close to the ferry wharf, with wonderful harbour views. Nearby Camp Cove is a beach and picnic spot. A 30-minute walk from the beach along the foreshore leads to South Head, one of the headlands at the entrance to Sydney Harbour. The views are spectacular.

Also accessible by ferry are **Kirribilli** – directly across the harbour from the city and also reached by foot over the Harbour Bridge – and **Balmain**, to the west of Circular Quay. Both places have lively café-and-restaurant strips and great harbour views from foreshore parks.

A quick trip by road from the city by bus or taxi is **Vaucluse House** (open Tues–Sun 10am–4.30pm; admission fee). This splendid, 15-room mansion, begun in 1803, has its own beach, and comes complete with mock-Gothic turrets and battlements. A short walk away, down Coolong Road, is **Nielsen Park**, a bushland reserve that has a popular beach, as well as a café. There are good harbourside walks here too.

Surf Beaches

Further afield, both north and south of Sydney, are kilometres of inviting beaches. **Manly** got its name when the first governor of the colony thought that the Aborigines sunning themselves on the beach looked manly. This pleasant resort, reached by ferry or Jetcat from Circular Quay, has back-to-back beaches – a sheltered harbour beach on one side, an ocean-facing surf beach on the other – that are linked by the Corso, a lively promenade full of restaurants and tables for picnickers.

The golden sands of Bondi, Australia's best-known beach

Beyond Manly, beaches stretch all the way to Sydney's northern limits. Among these are **Curl Curl** and **Dee Why** (which offer good surfing), **Collaroy** and **Narrabeen** (with sea pools ideal for families), and **Newport**, **Avalon** and **Whale Beach** (more good surfing).

At the northern tip of the Sydney beach region is **Palm Beach**, which is in a class of its own. The beautifully manicured gardens and villas of millionaires occupy the hills of the peninsula behind the beach. You can get to Palm Beach by taking the 190 bus from outside Wynyard railway station in the city centre; the trip takes about an hour.

Bondi (pronounced *bond-eye*), is a favourite with surfers and an Australian icon. The varied characters on the sand range from ancient sunworshippers to topless bathing beauties, and include quite a few British backpackers. Families tend to congregate at the northern end, where there is a wading pool. The beach gets very crowded on summer weekends. Set back from the beach, Bondi Pavilion has a café and bar, and is a good place for people-watching. Behind it is Bondi's main promenade and restaurant strip, Campbell Parade.

A string of lesser-known but lovely beaches stretches to the south of Bondi. These, including Tamarama, Clovelly, Bronte and Coogee, are well worth seeing, and can be reached on foot by a scenic coastal walking track that starts at the southern end of Bondi beach. It takes about an hour to walk to Bronte from Bondi; a half-hour extra for the Bronte to Coogee stretch.

Olympic Sydney

Since the 2000 Games, Sydney's magnificent, purpose-built Olympic Park has been somewhat under-employed. Critics call it a white elephant, but the Park is still fun to visit (<www.sydneyolympicpark.com.au>). The best way to get

ANZ Stadium was purpose-built for the 2000 Olympics

there is to catch a Parramatta Rivercat ferry from Circular Quay. These depart hourly and give a 50-minute scenic river trip before you alight at Olympic Park wharf.

The graceful, parabola-shaped centrepiece of Olympic Park, **ANZ Stadium** (hourly guided tours 10am–4pm), was Sydney's premier Olympic venue. It is now the venue for rugby league games and the occasional concert.

Not far away is **Sydney International Aquatic Centre** (SIAC; open Mon–Fri 5am–9pm, Sat–Sun 6am–8pm), which is open to the public. Besides its pools, the centre has five spas, a river ride, spray jets, spurting 'volcanoes', a water slide and a bubble beach.

Surrounding these and other venues are extensive parklands, good for gentle walks and picnics. There are also a small number of cafés and restaurants.

Excursions from Sydney

Within striking distance of Sydney – by car, train, or sightseeing bus – a choice of scene-changers shows the big variety of attractions offered by New South Wales. Any of the most popular outings will deepen your understanding of Australia and its assets.

Heading South

Thanks to a bit of historical gerrymandering, **Jervis Bay**, 200km (124 miles) south of Sydney, and 260km (161 miles) northeast of Canberra, is actually part of the Australian Capital Territory. The founders of Canberra *(see page 68)* annexed the area in the early 20th century on the off-chance that the future capital city might need a seaport. It didn't, however. The coastal enclave today includes an uncommon combination of facilities: inviting dunes and beaches rub shoulders with the Royal Australian Naval College, a missile range and Booderee National Park. Jervis, named after an English admiral, is correctly pronounced 'Jarvis', although locals are starting to rhyme it with nervous. The sand on Jervis Bay beaches is dazzling white and the sea is a crystal-clear blue. Dolphin cruises operate from the town of **Huskisson** (tel: (02) 4441 6311) – you almost always get to see dolphins, and sometimes migratory whales as well. Not far away, a delightful glade called **Greenpatch**, in Booderee National Park, offers some remarkably tame wildlife, including kangaroos, and multicoloured birds.

For more beautiful beaches and tame wildlife, head 95km (60 miles) south from Huskisson to idyllic **Murramarang National Park**, just before the town of Batemans Bay. There are cabins and camping grounds here, as well as walking trails.

The Blue Mountains

A 90-minute trip west of Sydney by road brings you to the **Blue Mountains**, a dramatic region of forested ravines and pristine bushland that has a World Heritage listing. The Blue Mountains offer a wealth of adventure activities, art and craft galleries, and romantic escapes in grand country lodges or cosy bed and breakfasts.

The name 'Blue Mountains' derives from the mountains' distinctive blue haze, produced by eucalyptus oil evaporating from millions of gum trees. Well-marked walking trails criss-cross Blue Mountains National Park, passing streams and waterfalls, descending into cool, impressive gorges, and snaking around sheer cliffs. This breathtaking environment is easily reached from Sydney, either by road or on a two-hour rail journey. Trains run there several times daily from Central Station.

The region's best-known rock formation is **The Three Sisters**, a trio of pinnacles best viewed from **Katoomba**, the largest of 26 mountain towns. The **Scenic Railway**, the world's steepest railway, descends from the cliff-top at Katoomba into the **Jamison Valley**. You can walk down a series of steps by the Three Sisters, stroll along a cool and refreshing trail and catch the Katoomba Scenic Rail to the top. Above, the **Scenic Skyway** carries passengers along a cableway 206m (675ft) above the valley floor. The **Scenic Cableway** descends over 500m (1,600ft) into the Jamison Valley.

For a less touristy view of the Blue Mountains, drive to the lookout at Govetts Leap, near **Blackheath**, 12km (7½ miles) west of Katoomba. The panorama is magnificent.

Of the numerous walking trails in the Blue Mountains, many involve a steep descent into a valley and a steep climb back to the top. For information about walks in the area, see <www.nationalparks.nsw.gov.au>.

For more than a century, spelunkers, hikers and ordinary tourists have admired the **Jenolan Caves**, at the end of a long, steep drive down the mountains west of Katoomba. Guided tours through the spooky but awesome limestone caverns

The vast Jamison Valley lies below the Three Sisters

last about an hour and a half. The atmosphere inside the caves is cool in summer, warm in winter, and always damp (for full information, tel: 1300 763 311; <www.jenolancaves.org.au>).

Ku-ring-gai Chase

North of Sydney is **Ku-ring-gai Chase National Park**. This area of unspoiled forests, cliffs and heathland fringing the Hawkesbury River, is home to numerous species of animals and birds. But you have to find them for yourself; it's not a zoo. There are also many good walking trails through untouched bushland. West Head Lookout, on top of a headland, gives outstanding views of the river and ocean. The Aborigines who lived in this area long before the foundation of New South Wales left hundreds of rock carvings – mostly pictures of animals and supernatural beings. The information centre at Bobbin Head Road, Mount Colah (tel: (02) 9472 8949) has maps pinpointing the locations of the most interesting carvings, as well as showing the park's network of trails.

Hunter Valley

Australia is one of the world's major wine-producing countries. The Hunter Valley, a two-hour drive from Sydney, is the premier wine-growing area of New South Wales. The Hunter's 60 or so wineries harvest grapes in February and March and welcome visitors throughout the year. The gateway to the Pokolbin region, where the majority of the Lower Hunter Valley wineries are located, is **Cessnock**, 195km (121 miles) north of Sydney. The tourist information centre, in the nearby town of Pokolbin, supplies touring maps and brochures, or you can join a day tour from Sydney.

Most of the Hunter wineries are open for cellar-door tastings. Some of the major establishments include Tyrell's, Lindemans, Wyndham Estate, Rosemount Estate, the Rothbury Estate and the McWilliams Estate.

Cape Byron, near Byron Bay, is Australia's most easterly point

Heading North

Newcastle, the commercial centre of The Hunter, is located approximately 170km (106 miles) to the north of Sydney. It's a coalmining and shipbuilding centre, and also offers well-developed recreational possibilities on the Pacific, the **Hunter River** and the huge saltwater **Lake Macquarie**. The lake, which is popular with weekend sailors and fishermen from far afield, is said to be the largest seaboard lake in Australia.

Further north, **Port Stephens** offers safe swimming beaches, a range of water activities and good fishing. Its bay is home to dozens of bottlenose dolphins, which can be viewed up close on a cruise.

In the far north of New South Wales, 790km (490 miles) from Sydney, **Byron Bay** provides wonderful beaches and great surf. Whale-watching boat trips offer an opportunity to see humpback whales when they migrate along the coast

here in June/July and September/October. The town is a haven for alternative lifestylers and millionaires.

Lord Howe Island

In the South Pacific, 483km (300 miles) east of Port Macquarie, Lord Howe Island, the state's off-shore possession, is the world's most southerly coral isle. This makes for splendid snorkelling and scuba diving. If you prefer to stay dry you can go out in a glass-bottom boat. There are also numerous walking trails, many birds and some unique vegetation.

Remote Lord Howe Island, home to some fabulous scenery

Forests, beaches, mountains and all, Lord Howe Island only amounts to a speck in the ocean – around 1,300 hectares (3,220 acres) – with a population of approximately 300 and a couple of cars. Bicycles and motorbikes are ideal for getting around as the roads are very quiet. You can fly out from Sydney or Brisbane in a couple of hours.

The Snowy Mountains

If you've come to Australia in search of snow, you need go no further than the southeastern corner of New South Wales. Skiing in the Snowy Mountains is usually restricted to the months of July, August and September. But even in the antipodean summer a few drifts of snow remain to frame the wild flowers of the Australian Alps. At the top of this world is **Mt Kosciuszko**, at 2,228m (7,308ft) high, named after an 18th-century Polish patriot by a 19th-century Polish explorer. This is the birthplace of three important rivers, the Murray, the Murrumbidgee and the Snowy.

Kosciuszko National Park is made up of approximately 6,300 sq km (2,432 sq miles) of the kind of alpine wilderness you won't see anywhere else: buttercups and eucalyptus and snow, all together in the same breathtaking panorama. The only thing missing is a pine tree, or any of the other familiar conifers of the Northern Hemisphere. There are many hiking trails for summer walks. Cars must be equipped with snow chains from 1 June to 10 October. However, even during the summer months the weather can change for the worse at very short notice, so be sure always to carry a warm, waterproof jacket. The best-known ski resorts in this area are **Thredbo** and **Perisher Valley**.

New South Wales Outback

Although New South Wales is the most populous and productive state (in both manufacturing and farming), it extends to the infinities of the Australian Outback.

Dubbo, a five-hour drive from Sydney, is the sort of place where the Old Gaol, meticulously restored, is a prime tourist attraction, gallows and all. Just out of town, the **Western Plains Zoo** (open daily 9am–5pm; <www.westernplainszoo.com.au>; admission fee) is Australia's only open-range zoo, a cageless convention of koalas, dingoes and emus, plus giraffes, zebras and monkeys.

Lightning Ridge, in the Back of Beyond near the Queensland border, enjoys one of the most evocative of Outback names. Fortune hunters know it well as the home of the precious **black opal**. Tourists are treated to demonstrations of fossicking, and there are opportunities to shop for opals.

Bourke is a small town on the Darling River whose name has come to signify the loneliness of the Outback, where dusty tracks are the only link between distant hamlets. 'Back of Bourke' is an Australian expression for a place that is extremely remote. Bourke looks a lot bigger on the map than on the ground.

Broken Hill (population around 20,000) is about as far west as you can go in New South Wales, almost on the border with South Australia. It's so far west of Sydney, there's a half-hour time difference, even though both are in the same state. The town is legendary for its mineral wealth – it has produced millions of tons of silver, lead and zinc. Tourists can visit the mines, either underground or on the top. The neatly laid-out town, with its streets named after various minerals – Iodide, Kaolin, Talc – has become an artistic centre, with works by Outback painters on show in numerous galleries. Pro Hart, one of Australia's best-known and most prolific painters, was a long-time Broken Hill resident. The School of the Air and the Royal Flying Doctor Service – both Outback institutions – give a further taste of life 'back of beyond'.

CANBERRA

When the new nation was proclaimed at the turn of the 20th century, the perennial power struggle between Sydney and Melbourne reached an awkward deadlock. Each of the cities offset its rival's claim to be the national capital. So they carved out a site in the rolling bush 300km (185 miles) south-west of Sydney, and it soon began to sprout clean, white, official buildings, followed by millions of trees and shrubs. Out of conflict emerged a green and pleasant compromise, far from the pressures of the big cities. Where sheep had grazed, the young Commonwealth raised its flag. As compromises go, it was a winner.

Designing the Capital

To design a model capital from scratch, Australia held an international competition. The prize was awarded in 1912 to the American architect Walter Burley Griffin. He had grand designs, but it took longer than anyone imagined to transfer his plan from the drawing board to reality, owing not only to the distractions of two world wars and the Depression, but also to a great deal of wrangling. Burley Griffin, a Chicagoan of the Frank Lloyd Wright school, put great emphasis on coherent connections between the settings and the buildings, and between landscape and cityscape.

Canberra, at the heart of the Australian Capital Territory, has a population of about 325,000. Although the city is an educational and research centre, it is essentially a company town – and the local industry is government. The ministries are here, and the parliament with its politicians, lobbyists and hangers-on, and so are the foreign embassies. The Royal Military College Duntroon, Australia's first military college, founded in 1911, is based in Canberra, as is the Australian National University and the Australian Institute of Sport. In spite of this considerable enterprise, Australia's only sizeable inland city is both uncrowded and relaxed.

Anzac Parade and, across the lake, Parliament House

City Sights

There are several good ways to see Canberra – but not on foot. The distances are greater than you think. If you do want to walk, many of the main attractions are found near Lake Burley Griffin – but you'll still need three or four hours. It's a good idea to sign up for a bus tour; they come in half-day and all-day versions. Or take a City Sightseeing bus, which runs a 25-km (15-mile) route stopping at all the main sights. You buy a 24-hour ticket, then hop on and off at will. Alternatively, you can drive yourself around the town or hire a bike, following itineraries that are mapped out in a free sightseeing pamphlet available from the Canberra Visitor Information Centre (Northbourne Avenue, Dickson; tel: (02) 6205 0044; <www.canberratourism.com.au>).

An effective starting place for a do-it-yourself tour is **Regatta Point**, which overlooks the man-made **Lake Burley Griffin**. Cleverly created in the middle of town the lake, 35km (22 miles) around, is generously named after the town planner who realised the value of water for recreation as well as scenic beauty. You can enjoy fishing, sailing and windsurfing here, or hop on a sightseeing boat with Southern Cross Cruises (tel: (02) 6273 1784). Whooshing up from the lake, a giant **water jet** honours the explorer Captain Cook for several hours each day (daily 11am–2pm). The **National Carillon**, another monument rising from Lake Burley Griffin (actually from a small island), was a gift from the British government. Apart from concert recitals, it tells the time every 15 minutes, taking its tune from London's Big Ben.

In a prime position at the tip of the Acton Peninsula is the **National Museum of Australia** (open daily 9am–5pm; <www.nma.gov.au>; free), a social history museum with themed galleries relating to the land, the people and the nation. The First Australians Gallery looks unflinchingly at the plight of the Aboriginal people after Europeans arrived,

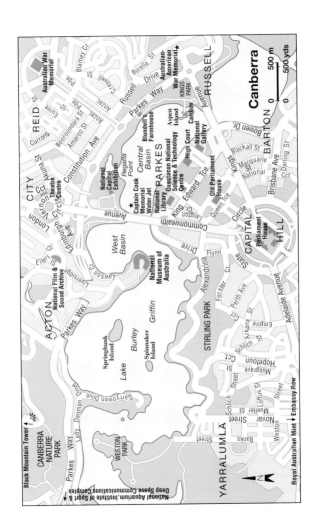

The National Carillon *(page 70)*

from the early massacres to the 20th-century government policy of taking Aboriginal children from their parents (the 'Stolen Generations'). There is plenty to see at this excellent museum.

North of the Lake

To get the best view of Canberra and surrounds, drive to **Black Mountain**. There are free lookouts here, or you can pay for a 360-degree perspective by going up the **Black Mountain Tower** (open daily 9am–10pm; admission fee), which stands 195m (640ft) high. A viewing platform circles the structure towards the top, and the designers couldn't resist adding a café and a revolving (and expensive) restaurant. If you want to eat there, you'll have to book ahead – tel: (02) 6248 6162.

On the eastern slopes of Black Mountain, the **National Botanic Gardens** (open daily 8.30am–5pm; <www.anbg. gov.au>) are entirely devoted to Australian flora – they have the most comprehensive collection anywhere. In spite of Canberra's mostly mild, dry climate, numerous rainforest specimens flourish under intensive care. Walter Burley Griffin was so fascinated by the native trees and plants of Australia that he included this place in his original plan.

The only part of the capital designed with pedestrians in mind is the area around the **Civic Centre**. The original business and shopping district opened in 1927 – by Canberra standards that's ancient history – and comes complete with symmetrical white colonnaded buildings in a mock-Spanish style. Nearby are modern shopping malls, the **Canberra Theatre Centre** on London Circuit, and an historic merry-go-round in Petrie Plaza.

A more conventionally styled dome covers the vast **Australian War Memorial**, which is a sandstone shrine climaxing a ceremonial avenue called **Anzac Parade**. There are war memorials all over Australia, but this is the definitive one. It's hard to avoid being swept up in the mood of the place as you walk past walls inscribed with the names of more than 100,000 Australian war dead. But beyond the statues and murals, the memorial is the most-visited **museum** in Australia (open daily 10am–5pm; <www.visitwarmemorial. com.au>; free). Items displayed in its 20 galleries include uniforms through the years, battle maps, and plenty of hardware, from rifles to a World War II Lancaster bomber.

Closer to the lake is one final military monument: the **Australian-American Memorial**, a slim aluminium shaft supporting a stylised eagle. It was paid for by public contributions in order to acknowledge US participation in the defence of Australia during World War II.

South of the Lake

The mostly windowless walls of the **National Gallery of Australia** (open daily 10am–5pm; <www.nga.gov.au>; free) were designed to enclose 'a museum of international significance,' as official policy decreed. The enterprise has succeeded on several levels, showing off artists as varied as Monet and Matisse, Pollock and de Kooning, along with an honour roll of Australian masters, including Tom Roberts, Arthur Streeton, Sidney Nolan, Arthur Boyd and Albert Tucker. Another indication of the range of interests represented here are the displays of art from Pacific island peoples, Africa, Asia and pre-Columbian America. The gallery also plays host to touring international exhibitions.

One of the high points of the National Gallery is the collection of Australian Aboriginal art: intricate human and animal forms on bark, evolving into the modern version in polymer paint on chipboard, dots and whorls and crosshatching looking at first glance like arbitrary abstractions. The gallery also has a glistening sculpture garden overlooking Lake Burley Griffin.

One of Canberra's best known landmarks is **Questacon**, the **National Science and Technology Centre** (open daily 9am–5pm; tel: (02) 6270 2800; <www. questacon.edu.au>; admission fee), a hands-on science museum that is very much geared towards children and teenagers. There are more than 200 exhibits in seven galleries. Architecturally, it's an interesting study in curves. The copper-plated dome rests on graceful arches standing in a circular moat. Some say it looks like a flying saucer at rest.

Also on the lakefront, the **National Library** (open daily 9am–9pm; <www.nla.gov.au>) houses more than 2 million books. This institution serves scholars and other libraries, and

What's in a Name?

The name of Australia's new capital city, which is said to be derived from 'meeting place' in an Aboriginal tongue, was officially chosen in 1913 from among a huge outpouring of suggestions. Some of the more serious citizens wanted to have a name as uplifting as Utopia or Shakespeare. Others devised classical constructions, for example Auralia and Austropolis. The most unusual proposal was a coinage designed to soothe every state capital: Sydmeladperbrisho. After that mouthful, the name Canberra came as a relief.

Australia's centre of government, Parliament House

mounts exhibitions of rare books. Its reading room houses an extensive selection of overseas newspapers and magazine publications. There are guided tours, a bookshop, and a café.

Canberra's neo classical **Old Parliament House** became the seat of government in 1927 and fulfilled that role until it was replaced in 1988. It is now the home of the **National Portrait Gallery** (open daily 9am–5pm; tel: (02) 6270 8236; <www.portrait.gov.au>; admission fee). Outside it is the **Aboriginal Tent Embassy**, erected to protest that Aboriginal land rights have not been achieved.

A new, permanent parliament building to replace the old one was dedicated by Queen Elizabeth II in the bicentennial year, 1988. **Parliament House** (open Mon–Fri 9am–5pm; tel: (02) 6277 5399; <www.aph.gov.au>; free guided tours) is worth a visit. The interior represents the best in Australian art and design. The Great Hall is dominated by a tapestry 20m (66ft) high. The combination of an unusual design as well as exploding building costs made the new complex a surefire *cause célèbre* during its construction. Taxpayers noted the lavish offices, bars, swimming pool and sauna.

Meanwhile, they're minting it in the southwestern district called Deakin, and you can take a look for yourself. The **Royal Australian Mint** (open Mon–Fri 9am–4pm, Sat–Sun 10am–4pm) has a visitors' gallery overlooking the production line where the country's coins are punched out. The factory also 'moonlights' to produce the coins of several other countries. The Mint's own museum contains coins and medals of special value.

Other Canberra attractions include the **National Film and Sound Archive** and the **Australian Institute of Sport**, which includes an interactive sports exhibition called Sportex. There are athlete-led guided tours of the Institute daily starting at 10am, 11.30am, 1pm and 2.30pm.

Out of Town

Animal lovers don't have far to go for a close encounter with kangaroos, echidnas, wombats and koalas. The **National Zoo and Aquarium** (open daily 9am–5pm; <www.national zoo.com.au>; admission fee) is only a few kilometres southeast of the city centre, in Yarralumla. You can walk through acrylic tunnels while sharks cruise past. The bird population includes parrots, kookaburras, cockatoos and emus.

The **Tidbinbilla Nature Reserve** (open daily 9am–6pm, 9am–8pm in summer; tel: 13 22 81), 40km (25 miles) southwest of Canberra, is a much bigger affair – thousands of hectares of bushland where kangaroos, wallabies and koalas flourish. Next to this unspoilt wilderness, the **Canberra Deep Space Communication Complex** (open daily 9am–5pm), one of only three deep-space tracking stations in the world, operated in conjunction with the US space agency NASA. The Complex has several exhibitions on space exploration.

QUEENSLAND

Queensland provides just about everything that makes Australia so desirable, plus some spectacular exclusives of its own. The sun-soaked state gives you the choice of flashy tourist resorts, Outback mining towns or a modern metropolis; rainforest, desert or apple orchard. But the most amazing attraction of all is Queensland's offshore wonderland – the longest coral reef in the world, the Great Barrier Reef.

Queensland was founded in 1824 as a colony for incorrigible convicts, the 'worst kind of felons', for whom not even the rigours of New South Wales were a sufficient deterrent. In an effort to quarantine criminality, free settlers were banned from an 80-km (50-mile) radius. But adventurers, missionaries and hopeful immigrants couldn't be held back for long. Queensland's pastureland attracted many eager squatters, and in 1867 the state joined the great Australian gold rush with a find of its own. Prosperity for all seemed to be just around the corner.

Another day in Surfers Paradise

Mining still contributes generously to Queensland's economy. Above ground, the land is kind to cattle and sheep, and warm-hearted crops like sugar, cotton, pineapples and bananas. But tourism is poised to become the biggest money-spinner, for Queensland is Australia's vacation state, welcoming tourists to wild tropical adventurelands in the far north, and the sophistication of the Gold Coast in the south. The busiest gateways to all of this are the state capital, Brisbane, and the port of Cairns, which has become one of Australia's most popular tourist destinations.

Brisbane

As befits a subtropical city with palm trees and back-garden swimming pools, **Brisbane** has a pace is so relaxed you'd hardly imagine its population is 1.8 million. The skyscrapers, some quite audacious, have gone a long way towards overcoming the 'country-town' image, but enough of the old, elegant, low-slung buildings remain as a reminder of former days; some are wonderful filigreed Victorian monuments, some done up in bright, defiant colours. As well as having its

The towers of Brisbane line the river

own attractions, the city is also a handy gateway to nearby tourist sites such as the Gold Coast and Fraser Island.

In 1859, when Brisbane's population was all of 7,000, it became the capital of the newly proclaimed colony of Queensland. The colonial treasury contained only 7½ pence, and within a couple of days even that was stolen. Old habits of the former penal colony seemed to die hard.

The capital's location, at a bend in the Brisbane River, has made possible some memorable floods over the years, but it sets an attractive stage for Australia's third-largest city. Spanned by a network of bridges (the first dated 1930), the river continues through the suburbs to the beaches and islands of Moreton Bay, 29km (18 miles) from central Brisbane. Some of Australia's most celebrated types of seafood come from here, notably the gargantuan local mud crabs and the Moreton Bay bug. Despite its unappealing name, this creature, related to the lobster, is a gourmet's joy.

Up the hill, on Wickham Terrace, stands an unusual historic building, the **Old Windmill**, also known as the Old Observatory, built by convicts in 1829. Design problems foiled the windmill idea; to grind the colony's grain, the energy of the wind had to be replaced by a convict-powered treadmill.

The nearby **Roma Street Parkland** is a diverse area of waterfalls, lakes, misty crannies of tropical vegetation, and floral displays with their own ecosystem of insects and birds. It is said to be the world's largest subtropical garden in a city.

King George Square, next to City Hall, and the nearby **Anzac Square**, are typical of the green open spaces that make the central business district (CBD) breathable. Pedestrians-only **Queen Street Mall** is flanked by big stores and interspersed with shady refuges and cafés. Here, on a fine day, visitors from cooler climes should take a seat to enjoy the warm sun and watch the passers-by. Or you can stroll along Albert Street, from King George Square to the City Botanic Gardens.

Brisbane's City Hall

Where central Brisbane fits into the bend in the river, the **City Botanic Gardens** (open 24 hours) turn the peninsula green with countless species of Australian and 'exotic' trees, plants and flowers. **Parliament House** (tours Mon–Fri 9am–4.15pm), built in the 19th century in Renaissance style, overlooks the gardens and is the headquarters of the state's legislative assembly.

Across the Goodwill footbridge from the Botanic Gardens or Victoria Bridge from the centre of town (and also accessible by ferry) is one of the city's main focal points, **South Bank**, a precinct of parks, gardens, restaurants, cafés and many other attractions stretching along the southern bank of the river.

At its northern end is the **Queensland Cultural Centre**, which puts most of Brisbane's cultural eggs in one lavish, modern basket. The Centre includes the **Queensland Art Gallery** (open Mon–Fri 10am–5pm, Sat–Sun 9am–5pm; <www.qag.qld.gov.au>; free), the **Gallery of Modern Art** (same hours as gallery; <www.qag.qld.gov.au/goma>; free), the **Queensland Museum** (open daily 9.30am–5pm; <www.southbank.qm.qld.gov.au>; free) and its offshoot **Sciencentre** (same hours as museum; admission fee), an interactive science museum aimed at kids and teens. Here too is the **Queensland Performing Arts Centre**, which has several performance spaces.

To the south of the Cultural Centre, and linked to it by a beautiful bougainvillea-clad arbour, are the **South Bank Parklands**. The attractions here include a market (Fri 5–10pm, Sat

10am–5pm and Sun 9am–5pm) and an artificial beach (**Streets Beach**). There is a diverse array of restaurants, making this is the place to head for on a sunny day, for an outdoor meal. Brisbane enjoys a reputation for chefs who make good use of their state's natural resources: mud crabs, avocados, macadamia nuts, mangoes, barramundi, coral trout and oysters, to name a few.

If you're looking for a classic Brisbane pub, check out the **Breakfast Creek Hotel**, built in 1889, on the north side of a bend in the Brisbane River, about 5km (3 miles) east of the CBD. If you seek bars and restaurants, **Fortitude Valley**, just outside the CBD, is a lively precinct. Brunswick Street, the valley's main thoroughfare, is lined with nightclubs, street cafés, ethnic restaurants and arty little shops. This suburb is also the location of Brisbane's **Chinatown**. At weekends a market operates. Nightlife there can be fun, but it's wise to

Streets Beach at South Bank

take a taxi when heading home after dark. Linking Fortitude Valley to Kangaroo Point is **Story Bridge**, a city landmark which you can climb on guided tours (tel: 1300 254 627).

To escape the heat and rush of the city, try **Mt Coot-tha Botanic Gardens** (open daily 8am–5pm), in Toowong, 7km (4 miles) west of the city centre. Covering 52 hectares (128 acres), these are the largest tropical and subtropical gardens in Australia. They feature a giant modern dome enclosing 200 species of tropical plants.

It's only about 11km (7 miles) to **Lone Pine Sanctuary** (open daily 8.30am–5pm; admission fee), one of the country's best-known collections of native animals. By boat from North Quay in the city centre the trip is several kilometres longer, taking 1½ hours. The stars of the show, of course, are the koalas, mostly sleeping like babies, clinging to their eucalyptus branches.

The islands of Moreton Bay, some unpopulated, make this a vast fishing and sailing paradise. **St Helena Island**, now a national park, became a penal settlement in the 1860s and remained a high-security prison until the 1930s; the excellent tours (to book, tel: (07) 3893 1240), setting out across the bay from Manly on the *Cat-O'-Nine Tails*, include a night-time ghost tour where actors re-enact scenes from the convict era. **Moreton Island** features **Mt Tempest**, at 285m (935ft) the world's highest stabilised coastal sand dune. On **North Stradbroke Island**, the Aboriginal community has developed a 90-minute tour called the **Goompi Trail**. An Aboriginal guide explains the flora and fauna, with Dreamtime stories, bush tucker (food) and traditional medicine.

Koala mascot

The koala is Queensland's official mascot. Its only occupation is eating eucalyptus leaves, the odour of which impregnate its whole body, providing both antiseptic protection and a deterrent to predators.

The Gold Coast

South of Brisbane, a day-trip distance if you're rushed, the **Gold Coast** is a Down Under impression of Miami Beach. Although it may be overexploited, it's so dynamic and there are such a lot of opportunities for things to do that you can hardly fault it. And the beach – anything from 30–50km (19–30 miles) of it, depending on who's doing the measuring – is a winner in any league. More than 20 Gold Coast surfing beaches patrolled by life-savers form the backdrop for activities such as swimming, sailing, boating, surfboarding and windsurfing.

Hold on tight at Movie World

The trip down the Pacific Highway south from Brisbane (78km/49 miles and roughly an hour's drive) is a study in Australian escapism. In the midst of forest and brushland grows a seemingly unending supply of amusement parks, luring fun-seekers with attractions for all the family: these diverting parks have names like Dreamworld, Sea World and Wet 'n' Wild. **Warner Bros Movie World** (open daily 10am–5pm; <http://movieworld.myfun.com.au>), one of the biggest, offers a Hollywood-style experience, including stunt shows, special effects and amusement rides.

The **Dreamworld** park (open daily 10am–5pm; <www.dreamworld.com.au>) operates an attraction claimed to be 'one of the fastest rides in the world', the Tower of Terror.

Surf's up at Surfers Paradise

Visitors flock to action-packed rides with names like Wipeout and Cyclone, watch adventure films on a huge screen or (if they want something quieter) cuddle a koala. Other Gold Coast theme-park attractions include **Sea World** (open daily 10am–5pm; <http://seaworld.myfun.com.au>), noted for its dolphin displays, and **Wet 'n' Wild** (open daily from 10am, closing times vary; <http://wetnwild.myfun.com.au>), which contains a giant wave pool, a white-water ride and a seven-storey speed slide.

Nature-lovers can also enjoy **Currumbin Wildlife Sanctuary** (open daily 8am–5pm; tel: (07) 5534 1266; <www.currumbin-sanctuary.org.au>), where masses of squawking rainbow lorikeets are fed each morning and evening. Other animals featured include koalas, kangaroos, Tasmanian devils, snakes and crocodiles. Currumbin is down towards the southern extremity of the Gold Coast, which ends at **Point Danger**. Beyond lies New South Wales.

The essence of the Gold Coast is **Surfers Paradise**, as lively as any seaside resort in the world and much addicted to high-rise living. When you're not sunbathing, swimming or surfing, you can go bungee jumping or just window-shop, eat out, socialise or wander through the malls, one of which, **Raptis Plaza**, is adorned by a full-scale replica of

Michelangelo's *David*. The pace is hectic, and the revelry never stops. To unwind, take a leisurely boat cruise along the Southport Broadwater or canals of Surfers Paradise. Another Surfers Paradise landmark, not far from Sea World, is **Palazzo Versace**, the world's first Versace Hotel, billed as 'six star' and filled with all kinds of designer trappings.

Surfers Paradise is approached through a thicket of petrol stations, fast-food outlets and motels – a reconstruction of the outskirts of many an American city, and in very similar taste. The conglomeration is skyscrapered in a peculiar way – essentially tall, slim apartment blocks interspersed with bungalows. The high-rise skyline of Surfer's must now rank with Ipanema, Miami and Cannes for architectural overkill.

The lush green backdrop to the Gold Coast is known as the Hinterland. The area encompasses luxuriant subtropical rainforests, waterfalls and bushwalking tracks, mountain villages and guest houses, craft galleries and cosy farm-stay accommodation. **Lamington National Park**, a World Heritage area, is well worth visiting and is an easy day-trip from Surfers Paradise.

The Sunshine Coast

For the beachy perfection of the Gold Coast with less commercialism (although they're working on it), try the resorts of the **Sunshine Coast**, north of Brisbane. Some of Australia's best surfing is hiding here.

See a koala at Currumbin

The resort closest to Brisbane, **Caloundra**, has a beach for every tide. The northernmost town on the Sunshine

Coast, **Noosa**, used to be a sleepy little settlement, and the weekend haunt of local farmers and fishermen. That was in the 1960s, before the surfers, then the trendsetters from Sydney and Melbourne arrived. However, it's still very laid back. **Noosa National Park**, a sanctuary of rainforest and under-populated beaches, occupies the dramatic headland that protects Laguna Bay from the sometimes squally South Pacific breezes. Fraser Island *(see page 89)* is easily reached from here.

This whole stretch is home to some of Queensland's most gorgeous coastline. Beaches such as those fronting the towns of **Maroochydore** and **Coolum** are gems.

Inland, the Sunshine Coast Hinterland is laden with plantations of sugar cane, bananas, pineapples and passion fruit. The area is also a centre of production of the prized macadamia nut. Above **Nambour**, the principal town of the Hinterland, is the Blackall Range, a remnant of ancient volcanic activity. Attractive Blackall towns such as **Montville** and **Maleny** offer crafts shops, cafés and tearooms.

To the south, just off the Bruce Highway near Beerwah, is **Australia Zoo** (open daily 9am–4.30pm; <www.australiazoo. com.au>; admission fee). Made famous by the late Steve Irwin, the zoo has a wide variety of Australian wildlife, as well as many exotic species, including elephants and tigers.

The Great Barrier Reef

Australia's biggest and most wonderful sight, the **Great Barrier Reef**, lies just below the ocean waves. Many millions of minuscule cells multiply relentlessly in fantastic shapes, growing into an infinite variety of forms – and colours from lettuce green to flaming crimson – to create the world's largest living phenomenon. The reef is home to 400 different types of coral. It stretches as far as you can see and beyond: more than 2,900km (1,430 miles) of submerged tropical gardens. In among them, the sea is sprinkled with hundreds of islands.

The Great Barrier Reef is home to hundreds of species of coral

The giant reef was proclaimed a marine park by the Australian Government in 1975, and placed on the World Heritage list in 1981, becoming the biggest World Heritage area in existence. It is now managed by the Great Barrier Reef Marine Park Authority (<www.gbrmpa.gov.au>).

Seen more intimately through a diver's mask, the reef is the spectacle of a lifetime, like being inside a boundless tropical fishbowl among the most lurid specimens ever conceived. The fanciful shapes of the coral, gently waving in the tide, might almost lull you to sleep. But not for long. A blazing blue-and-red fish darts into sight, pursuing a cloud of a thousand minnows. A sea urchin stalks past on its needles; a giant clam opens its hairy mouth as if sighing with nostalgia for its youth, a century ago.

In 1770 Captain Cook was exploring the eastern Australian coast and stumbled upon the Great Barrier Reef: the *Endeavour* was gored by an unsuspected outcrop of coral.

Patching the holes as best they could, the crew managed to sail across the barrier, and the vessel limped onto the beach at what is now Cooktown, where some major repairs had to be improvised.

There are many ways of appreciating the coral and its fishy visitors. You can stay dry in a glass-bottom boat, or join a brief cruise aboard a semi-submarine. Or descend into an underwater observatory at the Townsville **Reef HQ** *(see page 98)*, which includes what is claimed to be the world's largest coral reef aquarium. Equipped with just a mask, fins and snorkel you can get close to the underwater world, but the only way to blend totally with the environment is in a weightless state, diving as long and as deep as you please with scuba gear. If you're not a qualified diver you can take a crash course at many of the resorts. Organised excursions for advanced divers are also readily available.

Heading off to explore the reef

In some places the coral stands exposed, but visitors are asked not to walk over it, as that severely damages the living organisms.

Island types

Not all of the reef's islands are made of coral. In fact, most of the popular resort islands are the tips of off-shore mountains. True coral cays are smaller, flatter and more fragile.

The Reef Islands

The reef – actually a formation of thousands of neighbouring clumps of reefs – runs close to shore in the north of Queensland but slants ever further out to sea as it extends southwards. Hundreds of islands are scattered across the protected waters between the coral barrier and the mainland. More than a dozen have been developed into resorts, ranging from spartan to sybaritic. But only two resort islands – Heron and Green – are on the reef itself. From all the others you have to travel, by sea or air, from 5–70km (3–43 miles) to reach the main attraction. Here are some details about the character and facilities of the resorts of the Great Barrier Reef, heading from south to north:

Fraser Island is actually south of the Great Barrier Reef but it is close enough to it, and interesting enough, to rate inclusion in this list. About 120km (75 miles) long, Fraser is considered to be the largest sand island in the world, and is listed as a World Heritage site. But there's more than just sand: lakes, marsh, pine forest and rainforest. This is an unspoilt island for fishing, beachcombing and four-wheel-drive trekking, not swimming or coral dives. You can take excursions and flights to the island from Hervey Bay, or stay overnight at resorts, lodges, cabins or campsites.

Lady Elliot Island is a coral isle, part of the reef, but situated south of the Tropic of Capricorn. Activities centre on diving, swimming and windsurfing. The gateway airport is in Bundaberg, a sugar-producing town 375km (233 miles) up the coast from Brisbane, and day-trip flights include use of the island's resort.

Heron Island is heaven for divers. It's a small coral island right on the Great Barrier Reef. Amazing coral and hundreds of species of fish are waiting to be sighted just outside your door. Alternatively, nature-lovers can concentrate on the giant green turtles, which waddle ashore between mid-October and March to bury their eggs in the sand. Heron Island is also the goal of thousands of migrating noddy terns and shearwaters. A resort on the island accommodates up to 250 people. There are no day trips and no camping.

Great Keppel Island is one of the larger resort islands in area and in tourist population (there is even a youth hostel). The white beaches are gorgeous. The Great Barrier Reef is fully 70km (44 miles) away, but Great Keppel is surrounded by good local coral, and there's an underwater observatory. Its beaches are among the best in the resort islands. Great Keppel is also one of the cheapest islands to reach from the mainland – a return ferry trip from Rosslyn Bay costs around A$40. For other angles on the sea's secrets

Perils of the Deep – and the Shallows

Take care when you explore the Reef: some species of coral can cause very painful burns. The crown-of-thorns starfish may also be lying in camouflaged ambush for you: it has thousands of poisonous spines.

But between December and April, perhaps the greatest threat of all comes from the box jellyfish ('stingers'). In summer these small, transparent, almost invisible creatures swarm along the north Queensland coast in their thousands – and their sting can be fatal. All the popular beaches have stinger net enclosures, along with vinegar for medication in case a tentacle gets through, but you should always heed the warning signs and, to be on the safe side, stay out of the water during the stinger season.

in the area, rent a sailboard, catamaran, motorboat and/or snorkelling gear, or try water-skiing or parasailing.

Brampton Island, with a resort operated by the Voyages company, is reached by air or sea from Mackay. With forested mountains and abundant wildlife, the island's mountainous interior is worth seeing. You can also discover neighbouring Carlisle Island, uninhabited and connected to Brampton by a reef that is

Hamilton Island chapel

wadeable when the tide's out. If the many sandy beaches don't suffice, there's a saltwater pool.

Lindeman Island is the most southerly of the islands in the Whitsunday archipelago, which was named by Captain Cook after the feast of Pentecost, approximately the time of year when he passed through. Lindeman Island was almost overrun by feral goats, but they have been eradicated. If you want an all-inclusive vacation you can stay at the Club Med Resort there. There's a campsite as well. Travel there by boat from Shute Harbour or fly from Hamilton Island *(below)*.

With its jet airstrip, large marina, 14-storey apartment tower, restaurants, bars and swimming pools, **Hamilton Island** is the slickest international resort in the Coral Sea. There are hotel rooms, apartments and bungalows for all budgets. Away from the main resort is Qualia, aimed at the top end of the market. Wherever you stay, divers can go out to the reef by catamaran or helicopter. The island's rainbow lorikeets not only eat out of your hand but sit on your arm while

For a taste of paradise try one of the Whitsunday islands

doing it. There are tame kangaroos, too. You can fly to
Hamilton Island from Sydney, Melbourne, Brisbane or Mackay, or fly to Proserpine and take a boat from Shute Harbour.

Long Island is 11km (7 miles) long – narrow and hilly.
Close to the mainland and far from the reef, it has three
resorts: Club Crocodile Long Island, Peppers Palm Bay and
South Long Island Nature Lodge. There's also a campsite.
Most of the island is national park rainforest.

South Molle Island also consists mainly of national park,
plus a resort. South Molle is virtually joined to North Molle
Island 2km (1¼ mile) away, and to the closer Mid Molle Island.
The beaches are good (there are some quiet ones at the south),
and you'll find nice paths for walks. The Great Barrier Reef is
about 60km (37 miles) away but coral reefs exist nearby.

Daydream Island is the tiniest of all the Barrier Reef resort
islands, snoozing just offshore from busy Shute Harbour.
Since beaches are not the island's strongest selling point, Day-

dream Island Resort and Spa has built swimming pools. The resort accommodates 300 guests.

Hayman Island, the most northerly of the Whitsunday group, boasts the chic, expensive international-class Hayman Island Resort, a lavish, five-star hotel. Hayman has a marina for drop-in yachts, and a choice of restaurants, bars and shops. The long, sandy beach suggests all sorts of watersports, dutifully organised for guests by the resort's activities staff. Some tiny, uninhabited isles are so close you can walk out to them at low tide. No day-trips to Hayman are available.

Magnetic Island is virtually a suburb of Townsville, the biggest city in northern Queensland. Many of the island's 2,000 or so permanent residents commute to work on the mainland by ferry. Being so easy to reach, it's a busy day-trip destination – by sea or helicopter – but Magnetic Island also has plenty of accommodation of all classes. Most of the island is a national park, busy with birds and other animals (including koalas in the eucalyptus trees), and the choice of beaches is enticing. Magnetic Island, 'Maggie' to the locals, was given its name by Captain Cook, whose compass malfunctioned here.

Famous visitors to **Orpheus Island** have included Zane Grey and Vivien Leigh half a century ago. Over 100 species of fish and 340 of the 350 known species of Reef coral adorn underwater gardens in the island's several sheltered bays, with the channel at the southern point of Orpheus believed to host the Reef's largest range of soft corals. The island is a national park, and Orpheus Island Resort is the sole resort. Nestling in a sheltered bay on the western (mainland) side of the island, the resort accommodates a maximum of 42 guests in 21 private rooms. Day-trippers and children under 15 are banned.

Hinchinbrook Island basks in a superlative of its own: 'The world's largest island national park'. A continental rather than coral island, but only 5km (3 miles) from the reef,

Hinchinbrook has a couple of campsites (park rangers issue permits on the mainland) and a small resort with 65 rooms. Inland from the smooth sand beaches, you will find mountains well worth climbing, as well as rainforest, waterfalls and bushland, where you'll come across wallabies. Day-trips to the island depart from Cardwell.

Bedarra Island, in the Family Islands group, accessible via neighbouring Dunk Island, has a very small, exclusive and pricey resort, operated by the Voyages company, on its west coast. You'll need a healthy bank balance to stay here. The nearest mainland town is Tully, noted for having the highest average annual rainfall in the country.

Dunk Island is mostly a national park, but one of the best developed resorts fits inoffensively into a corner of the island originally occupied by a World War II radar station. It's reached by ferry from Clump Point at Mission Beach. Dunk's genuine tropical rainforest offers a taste of the eternal: vines struggling to grab the sunlight at the expense of the trees they strangle on the way up. All is silence except for a waterfall, the trickle of raindrops off glistening leaves, the fluttering wings of a brightly plumed bird.

In the interior you can visit the carefully tended grave of Edmund Banfield, the island's first white resident. A journalist from Townsville, Banfield went to the island in 1898 to die quietly, having been given only weeks to live. He survived for 25 more years, writing books with titles including *The Confessions of a Beachcomber* and *My Tropic Isle*.

Kayaks for hire

Fitzroy Island came into the resort business later than most. It's only 6km (4 miles) offshore and easily reached on day excursions from Cairns. Lodging here is quite limited, but affordable, and a dining room and regular evening entertainment keep the overnight population, many of them backpackers, well amused. Fitzroy has some coral reef, and has rainforest in the interior; the beaches meet anyone's standards, however high. Nudey Beach is one of the best.

Tropical Dunk Island

Green Island, one of the two resorts actually on the reef, is, like Fitzroy, popular with day-trippers from Cairns, but when the crowds depart, the vacationers occupying the five-star Green Island Reef Resort have the tiny island, and its throngs of seabirds, to themselves. The resort has 46 suites. The Underwater Observatory, which claims to be the first of its kind in the world, lets you view the coral garden from the dry, some three fathoms below water level. In this situation, the fish come to look through the glass at human beings in the tank. Another attraction, just a short walk inland, is Marineland Melanesia, with crocodiles, stingrays, giant turtles, as well as Melanesian artefacts.

Lizard Island, a national park, situated about 30km (19 miles) off the tropical northern coast of Queensland, has all the trappings of a fictional escape island, with rainforest, mangrove swamps and a couple of dozen delectable beaches. The island is almost on the edge of one of Australia's most productive game-fishing zones, in which the half-ton black marlin are found. It's favoured by millionaires and celebrities, who stay at the exclusive and pricey Lizard Island Resort. The only other alternative is at the other end of the price scale: a very basic campsite. The island is reached by air from Cairns.

The Tropical Coast

The coast of mainland Queensland that is parallel to the Barrier Reef terminates in the north with Cape York Peninsula, one of Australia's wildest and least populated areas. If you're heading there, it's best to go with an experienced operator – roads are often little more than dirt tracks. Here are a few highlights further south, from south to north, heading along the Capricorn Coast relentlessly towards the Equator.

Rockhampton sits only a few kilometres north of the Tropic of Capricorn – 23°27' south of the Equator, and the line that officially divides the tropics from the subtropics. From here on northwards, you need no excuse to order an icy beer to assuage your tropical thirst. Rockhampton, known as the beef capital of Australia, has some genuinely interesting Victorian architecture, and is worth a walking tour. To the north, the Berserker Range offers spectacular limestone caves.

Mackay is the next substantial town, and even by Australian standards it's a long haul – about 340km (210 miles) – over Highway 1, a road not particularly noted for its scenery. Surrounded by dense fields of cane, Mackay processes one-third of the nation's sugar crop. At the harbour stands the world's biggest bulk sugar terminal. From July to December you can see cane crushing in progress at the **Farleigh Sugar Mill**, about 12km (7 miles) northwest of the town on the Bruce Highway. One of the largest national parks in Queensland, **Eungella National Park**, lies inland from Mackay, in rugged mountain country. There are many walking tracks, ranging in difficulty from easy strolls to strenuous hikes. This is one of the few places in Australia where you can see platypuses in the wild. The best time is morning and late afternoon and there's a platypus viewing platform near the bridge in Eungella township. **Proserpine**, another sugar town, is situated inland from **Airlie Beach** and **Shute Harbour**, resorts from which there are boat trips to the Whitsunday Islands.

Another 265km (165 miles) closer to the Equator, you reach the metropolis of Queensland's far north, **Townsville** (population 160,000). Townsville is the hub of the mining and cattle industries of Queensland's interior and one of the gateways for islands of the Reef, including neighbouring Magnetic Island *(see page 93)*. In the historic town centre, along the river, are some photogenic old buildings with filigreed iron balconies or stately columns and arches.

Cooling off in Townsville

One of Townsville's top attractions is **Reef HQ** (open daily 9.30am–5pm; <www.reefhq.com.au>; admission fee), with a superb simulation of the Great Barrier Reef, an IMAX cinema, and a colossal aquarium. Right next door, the **Museum of Tropical Queensland** (open daily 9.30am–5pm; <www.mtq. qm.qld.gov.au>; admission fee) combines maritime archaeology and the natural history of North Queensland. There's also a beachside playground along the 5-km (3-mile) **Strand**, adjoining Jupiters Casino and a water park playground.

The landscape changes from dry to lush as you head north to **Cairns**, Townsville's regional rival. Cairns (population over 122,000) rivals Townsville as Australia's largest tropical city. A port laid out in grid style with huge blocks and extra-wide streets, Cairns has benefited economically from Australia's tourist boom and grown dramatically, but in the process has lost much of its former sleepy, tropical outpost atmosphere. In a prominent position on Trinity Inlet is **The Pier** (a shopping and leisure complex), which fronts a large marina from which reef cruises and game-fishing excursions depart. The centrepiece of the waterfront, called the **Esplanade**, is a huge landscaped swimming lagoon. A large shopping complex, **Cairns Central**, is located just past Shields Street.

Cairns makes an ideal base, within reach of the Great Barrier Reef, the World Heritage-listed Daintree rainforest, the temperate Atherton Tableland, the Outback and even Cape York. Hundreds of tour options are available, and the city has become Australia's centre for adventure tourism. From hot-air balloon and bungee-jumping to skydiving and whitewater rafting, you can do it here.

Cairns action begins early in the morning, when speedy catamarans leave for Green Island and Fitzroy Island and smaller boats set sail with scuba divers or fishermen aboard. Big-game fishing for black marlin is big business in Cairns. Some travel agencies open their doors at 7.30am and keep going until after dark. They sell a large collection of excursions – to Green Island, inland to Kuranda and the Atherton Tableland, and up the coast as far as Port Douglas.

The town of **Kuranda**, 'the village in the rainforest', is a short distance northwest of Cairns. It is very tourist-oriented, with numerous craft shops, galleries, restaurants and two markets (one held daily 9am–3pm, the other on Wed, Thur, Fri, and Sun 9am–3pm). Kuranda is linked to Cairns by two fascinating transport systems: the wonderfully quaint and picturesque **Kuranda Scenic Railway**, and the **Skyrail Rainforest Cableway**, which transports visitors to Kuranda in six-person aerial gondolas over dense, tangled rainforest. You can buy tickets for a round trip – train one way and Skyrail the other. Skyrail riders can enter the forest on boardwalks at two stations on the way up and view trees from there. A rainforest information and research centre is located at Barron Falls Station. The Skyrail experience is even better when it's misty or raining and the gondolas fill with a woody aroma as mists rise from below. Sweeping views of sugarcane plantations, the Coral Sea, beaches and offshore islands give way to eucalyptus forest and later to the huge fig trees, kauri pines and twisted vines of the 120-million-year-old rainforest.

The Kuranda Scenic Railway more than lives up to its name

Daintree River crocodile

The **Tjapukai Aboriginal Cultural Park** at the base of Skyrail is home to the renowned Tjapukai Aboriginal Dance Theatre, which showcases the culture of the rainforest people of Tropical North Queensland. Performances are primal and electrifying (for bookings, tel: (07) 4042 9900).

Beautiful coastal scenery is the reward along the highway north from Cairns to **Port Douglas**. The town's palm-fringed Four Mile Beach is most people's idea of a tropical paradise. Once a little fishing village, Port Douglas has climbed on the tourism bandwagon, but it's more relaxed than Cairns. The fancy **Sheraton Mirage Resort** is the flashiest hotel in town. Near it, Quicksilver (<www.quicksilver-cruises.com>) runs catamaran services to the islands and outer reef.

Popular destinations near Port Douglas are the sugar-milling town of **Mossman**, **Daintree National Park**, with its World Heritage-listed rainforests, and lovely **Cape Tribulation**, where, as the tourist brochures say, 'the rainforest meets the sea'. There are also crocodile-spotting boat tours on the Daintree River. From Mossman north it's several hundred hot kilometres to the likeable river port of **Cooktown**, where Captain Cook's battered *Endeavour* was beached in 1770. The James Cook Memorial Museum tells all about it.

The tip of **Cape York Peninsula**, north of Cooktown, is a vast expanse of marshy terrain, prone to flooding and rife with crocodiles, only negotiable in well-equipped four-wheel-drive vehicles. The rivers are impassable from December to March; **Coen** is the last place for supplies and fuel.

NORTHERN TERRITORY

On the surface, the Northern Territory might seem an unpromising tourist destination. Its deserts, torrid tablelands and rainforests look immensely uninviting, and the region is especially discouraging when it's blazing hot. However, the wildlife is enchanting, the scenery is magnificent and the people, though few and far between, welcome the wandering stranger with Outback hospitality and charm.

The population totals only around 210,000. Their median age is 30 years, the youngest of any Australian state or territory. About one in three Territorians is an Aborigine, so cultural insights are part of the agenda for foreign visitors. This is the place to find the grandeur and mystery of the most sacred Aboriginal sites.

The Northern Territory covers about one-sixth of Australia's total area. Perhaps surprisingly, roads in 'NT' are generally of a high standard and a four-wheel-drive vehicle is not necessary unless you specifically want to pursue off-road activities. The climate divides the land into two parts: the north, called 'the Top End', is lush, monsoonal, and very hot and humid. The rest of the Territory, known as 'the Centre', has drastically less rainfall and very hot, dry summers.

Exploring 'the Centre'

Darwin

Australia's northernmost port, the capital of the Northern Territory, is a young, prosperous city radiating the optimism of the reborn, for **Darwin** has survived far more than its share of catastrophes. It was bombed scores of times in World War II. Rebuilt after the war, it was once again wiped out by Cyclone Tracy in 1974. Subsequently planners went back to the drawing board to design a bigger and better city.

The 114,000 Darwinians include more than 50 different ethnic groups, including a large Chinese community. This is reflected in the city's wide range of Asian and Western eating-places, ranging from up-market restaurants to budget-priced food stalls at the **Mindil Beach Sunset Markets** (Apr–Oct Thur 5–10pm, Sun 4–9pm).

Darwin's daytime temperature averages above 30°C (86°F) all year and the humidity can be debilitating. But while transients wilt, the locals know how to withstand the tropical conditions. They dress lightly and casually – even businesspeople wear shorts to work – they use air-conditioning and they drink a record amount of beer to quench their thirst. Although elsewhere in Australia a stubby means a small bottle of beer, order one in Darwin and you get a 2-litre bottle – almost half a gallon. This gives a clue to the Darwin sense of humour; and the jokes are nearly always a pleasant distraction from the heat. Empty beer cans often end up as the construction material for a flotilla of fanciful boats which compete in Darwin's annual slapstick regatta.

The Ghan train

A leisurely way to get to Darwin is by the Ghan, one of Australia's great trains. Run by Great Southern Railways (<www.gsr.com.au>) from Adelaide, the Ghan travels twice a week to Darwin (the 48-hour, two-night trip includes stopovers in Alice Springs and Katherine), as well as twice weekly overnight to Alice Springs.

Darwin's Parliament House was opened in 1994

Local chauvinists will admit that Darwin, about 4,000km (2,500 miles) from Sydney and Perth, is 'a trifle isolated'. But that doesn't deter the eager newcomers arriving from all parts of the country – not least for such adventurous activities as bungee jumping, parachuting and bush walking.

City Sights

Historic buildings are the last things you'd expect to find in a city wiped out by a modern cyclone. But visitors can tour the restored 19th-century buildings that bring to mind the atmosphere of the pioneering days. The old **Government House**, overlooking the harbour, is an elegant example of colonial style (opened in 1883). Although a series of cyclones and the wartime bombs badly damaged the building (known as the Seven Gables), it has been put back together in fine form, and is surrounded by lovely tropical gardens. It replaced an earlier building which was eaten by termites. In

The old Government House

turn, it has been replaced as the regional seat of government by a new **Parliament House**, opened in 1994.

Dating from 1885, the stone building known as **Browns Mart** is now a theatre. The building has a chequered past. Built as a miner's exchange, it was converted for use as a police station and subsequently served the community as a brothel.

Also on an offbeat historical theme, the **Fannie Bay Gaol Museum** (open daily 10am–4.30pm) opened for business in 1883. Closed down in 1979, the jail allows visitors to follow the advance of penal progress since those rough-and-ready days. The gallows were last used in 1952.

Other restored buildings include the **Victoria Hotel** (built in 1894), and the former **Admiralty House** (now a restaurant), raised high on stilts in tropical style. A surviving portion of the old Anglican **Christ Church Cathedral** has been incorporated into the modern building.

At the harbour, the **Darwin Waterfront** precinct is undergoing a major renovation. Apartments, a convention centre, parks, a lagoon and a beach are taking shape on old industrial land. Meanwhile, dozens of restaurants have set up tables at the end of the pier. The precinct also houses the **Indo-Pacific Marine Exhibition** (live coral displays) and the **Australian Pearling Exhibition**.

Yachts and other pleasure boats dock on the western side of Darwin, at **Cullen Bay Marina**. Boats leave here for popular daily sunset cruises of Darwin Harbour. There are also shops and restaurants.

Back in town, **Smith Street Mall** is a pedestrian-only shopping area, the retail heart of the city. The shady mall, with its stores, cafés and restaurants, is the perfect place for people-watching. All kinds of city and rural 'locals' congregate in the mall. Nearby **Mitchell Street**, lined with bars, pubs, cafés, restaurants, hotels and motels, is the city's nightlife hub.

Walk along Bennett Street to Woods Street to see the **Chinese Temple**. Notwithstanding its sweeping roofs, the building is guaranteed cyclone-proof. It serves Buddhists, Taoists and Confucians.

The **Museum and Art Gallery of the Northern Territory** (open Mon–Fri 9am–5pm, Sat–Sun 10am–5pm; tel: (08) 8999 8264; free) at Fannie Bay is worth a visit for its Aboriginal art section and the exhibition commemorating Darwin's destruction by Cyclone Tracy on Christmas Eve 1974. It killed more than 50 people. Another popular exhibit is the stuffed body of 'Sweetheart', a 5-m (16½-ft) saltwater crocodile.

A building that looks remarkably ambitious for a town of Darwin's size is **SkyCity Darwin**, a gleaming white pyramid of a leisure and casino complex overlooking Mindil Beach. Punters have a choice of traditional games in the sophisticated mould of Monte Carlo or the more folksy Australian style. You can try your hand at two-up, the Australian game that's as simple as tossing two coins.

Lovers of tropical flowers will be delighted by every little garden around town, but the ultimate display occupies the **George Brown Darwin Botanic Gardens**, 41 hectares (101 acres) of the most fetching flowers and plants. In addition to the bougainvillea and frangipani, the orchids are a special source of pride.

Back to the seaside for something completely different: Doctor's Gully Road, at the end of the Esplanade, is the site of a strange audience-participation ritual, the feeding of the fish. At **Aquascene**, tourists wade into the sea at high tide (check the local paper for the time or call (08) 8981 7837) to hand-feed catfish, mullet, bream, milkfish and other sizeable denizens of the harbour. Hundreds of fish turn up here daily, returning to deep-sea pursuits until the next handout.

Crocodylus Park (open daily 9am–5pm; <www.crocodylus park.com>; admission fee), a 15-minute drive east from the city centre, is home to around 1,000 crocodiles. The feeding sessions (at 10am, noon, 2pm and 3.30 pm) are very impressive, so try to time your visit to coincide with one.

South and East of Darwin

About 120km (75 miles) south of Darwin, off the Stuart Highway, is **Litchfield National Park**, which covers about 1,500 sq km (580 sq miles) of tropical savannah wilderness. There are rocky escarpments, waterholes for swimming, waterfalls, patches of monsoon forest and short walking trails. Here, as in Kakadu National Park *(see page 107)*, you can see '**magnetic anthills**', which are found scattered like dolmens in the bush. To be accurate, these are neither magnetic nor anthills. They are termite mounds, often taller than people, and are always aligned exactly north–south, for reasons unknown to scientists. They look like two-dimensional sandcastles.

Fogg Dam Conservation Reserve, 60km (37 miles) east of Darwin, off the Arnhem Highway, is a splendid sanctuary where a dozen species of water bird coexist on magical pools. A few kilometres further east you can take a **Jumping Crocodile Cruise** (tel: (08) 8978 9077) on the Adelaide River and watch as crocodiles leap vertically from the water next to your cruise boat, attracted by chicken meat dangled over the side by crew members.

Kakadu National Park

'Magnetic' termite mounds always point north–south

Birdwatchers, photographers and all other visitors are enthralled by **Kakadu National Park** (entrance fee for a 7-day pass). The park covers 19,800 sq km (7,200 sq miles), and the accommodation and commercial centre is Jabiru, 250km (155 miles) southeast of Darwin. The scenery ranges from romantic to awesome. As an unparalleled outdoor museum of ancient Aboriginal art, the park is on the Unesco World Heritage List of places of 'outstanding universal value'. Some of the paintings have been here since the era of Europe's Palaeolithic cave art.

Nineteen different clans of Aboriginal peoples live between the Wild Man and East Alligator rivers. They lease the land to the National Parks and Wildlife Service and participate in the park's daily management, including working as park rangers.

Nature has neatly divided Kakadu into two worlds: the plains, with their lagoons and creeks, and the escarpment, a stark sandstone wall marking the western edge of Arnhem Land. From the top of the high plateau waterfalls tumble to the lowlands in the wet season (November–March). The floodplains entertain water birds by the thousand. Their names alone are enticing enough to turn laymen into dedicated birdwatchers: white-throated grasswren, white-lined honeyeater and white-breasted whistler, to list but three of the species that breed in the park. The star of the show, though, is the jabiru, a stately variety of stork. In the mangroves you'll see striated heron, little kingfisher, broad-billed flycatcher and possibly also magpie goose, black shag, ibis and crested plover. A special delight is the sight of the delicately poised lotus bird, which seems miraculously to walk on the water. The waterways are rich in the eminently edible barramundi. Less appetisingly, the estuaries are home to the saltwater crocodile, a vicious predator which preys on barramundi, birds, small animals and, sometimes, human beings.

Kakadu's rock paintings feature stick figures in violent action

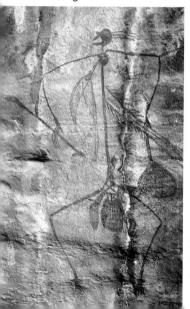

Kakadu's Rock Art
At as many as five thousand different places in the park – most notably at Nourlangie and Ubirr rocks – ancient Australians left works of art, rock paintings in styles both primitive and eerily sophisticated. The earliest legacy consists of handprints and the imprints of objects that were dyed and thrown at cliff walls and cave ceilings for decorative effect. Many centuries later, the abstract-expressionists reinvented a similar technique.

The next generation of prehistoric artists concentrated on depicting the figures of animals. Among them is a curious variety of anteater believed to have become extinct perhaps 18,000 years ago, a valuable clue to the age of some of these paintings. The same school of artists painted stick-figure humans in hunting and battle scenes using ochre pigments for colour.

Later artists introduced movement, such as hunters throwing boomerangs or spears. An innovation of this era was the employment of abstract marks around certain figures, like a modern cartoonist's squiggles representing a character's surprise or fear.

Thousands of years later, Aboriginal artists developed a remarkable style, now called X-ray painting. The profile of, say, a fish is clearly painted but instead of its scales we see its bones and internal organs, with the emphasis on edible or otherwise useful parts. After Australia was colonised, Europeans became a subject for the artists. There are pictures of British sailing ships and caricatures, scarcely flattering, of the new settlers holding recognisable muskets.

Katherine Gorge

The most spectacular natural attraction located at the Top End of the Northern Territory, **Katherine Gorge** is approximately 350km (217 miles) 'down the Track' from Darwin. The Track is what they call the highway linking the Timor Sea and Alice Springs in the Red Centre of Australia. Originally a rough path fit only for bullock carts and camel trains servicing the overland telegraph line, the route was upgraded by American servicemen during World War II to supply Darwin, which at the time was dangerously isolated and under Japanese attack.

Katherine, which is part of the **Nitmiluk (Katherine Gorge) National Park**, is not a single gorge but a series of 13. In the wet season (Nov–Mar) the torrents, waterfalls, whirlpools and rapids give an impression of thundering power, but it is very hot and humid, and sometimes the rains cut off the roads, so is best visited in the dry season (Apr–Oct), when the water flows at a relative trickle. Flat-bottomed boats cruise along the river, mostly on the lower two canyons, where the water reflects sheer cliffsides, but more inquisitive travellers can explore the other 11 canyons upstream either by hiring a canoe or swimming. Walks and hikes offer other perspectives. The Visitor Information Centre in Katherine (tel: (08) 8972 2650) will book tours.

Among the sights are Aboriginal wall paintings portraying kangaroos and other native animals, bigger than life-size. Live kangaroos may be seen in the park, as well as the echidna (spiny anteater) and the dingo. Adding a tremor of excitement is the possibility of glimpsing a freshwater variety of crocodile called Johnstone's Crocodile. Unlike the 'salties' of the north, though, these fierce-looking reptiles are timid fish-eaters; fortunately, tourists do not figure on their menu. Bird life is colourful and includes hooded parrots and black cockatoos. Katherine is also home to a Savannah Guide Station (<www.savannah-guides.com.au>): the eco-accredited specialist guides focus on heritage, culture, and preservation of the environment.

Alice Springs

Traffic lights have slightly tamed the adventurous Outback atmosphere of **Alice Springs**, the biggest town in the Red Centre, 1,500km (930 miles) south of Darwin. 'The Alice' still looks rather like the frontier town you imagined: a relaxed, friendly, slightly dishevelled community of pioneers, dreamers, transients and, more recently, throngs of tourists.

The Northern Territory's second biggest population centre has 24,000 inhabitants. When it comes to climate, they are extremists. In the summer it gets as hot as 42°C (108°F) but, mercifully, the nights in June, July, September and October require a sweater or two. Chances of seeing rain

Alice Springs, with the MacDonnell Ranges in the distance

are slight. The Henley-on-Todd Regatta (<www.henleyon
todd.com.au>), a whimsical fixture each August or September, is run on the sandy bed of the sometime Todd River,
a wide *wadi* gullying through the centre of town. The boats,
of many classes, are all bottomless and propelled by the racing legs of their crews.

The Alice first grew around a waterhole discovered in
1871 by the surveying party stringing the first telegraph line
from Adelaide to Darwin – and from there to the rest of the
world. Alice Springs was named after Alice Todd, who was
the wife of South Australia's postmaster general. He won
himself a knighthood for pushing through the project; locally,
the Todd River immortalises him.

Camels, traditionally ridden by experts from Afghanistan,
brought the equipment for the telegraph relay station built
at Alice Springs and the supplies to keep the technicians
alive. When termites devoured the first telegraph poles,

Aboriginal art for sale in
Alice Springs

replacements – heavy iron poles brought in from Britain – also had to be transported by camel train. Telegraphic messages aside, Alice Springs remained isolated until World War II – and until the 1960s it was little more than a crossroads market town. In February 2004 the Alice to Darwin 1,420-km (880-mile) railway extension was completed, fulfilling a century-old promise of a key economic and tourism link.

Like many an Australian town, The Alice is bigger than you might expect, but the essential sights can be taken in on a walking tour. The main street, **Todd Mall**, is lined with galleries selling Aboriginal art and craft. Here, too, is the **John Flynn Memorial Church**, dedicated to the founder of the flying doctor service, and **Adelaide House Museum** (tel: (08) 8952 1856 for opening hours; free), the town's first hospital.

The **Todd Tavern** at the top of Todd Mall is the town's liveliest drinking spot. There's also an 'international standard' casino, **Lasseters**, on Barrett Drive.

The **Royal Flying Doctor Service** (tel: (08) 8952 1129 for guided tours), which brings health care to the furthest cattle station, began in Alice Springs in 1928. You can visit the base, on the south side of town. Opposite the RFDS is the **Alice Springs Reptile Centre** (open daily 9.30am–

5pm; admission fee). Another service that eased development of the Outback, the **School of the Air** (open Mon–Sat 8.30am–4.30pm, Sun 1.30–4.30pm; admission fee), a radio, phone and internet link with isolated pupils, has its Visitor Centre on Head Street.

A couple of kilometres north of town, an unspoiled park surrounds the restored **Telegraph Station** (tel: (08) 8952 3993 for information on guided tours). This was the most important relay station on the line. Before the wires were strung a message could take three months to reach London from Adelaide. The relics here give a glimpse of 19th-century technology and the lonely life of the telegraph pioneers.

A couple of kilometres west of town along Larapinta Drive is the **Alice Springs Cultural Precinct** (open Mon–Fri 10am–4pm, Sat–Sun 11am–4pm; admission fee), a group of museums and galleries. The **Araluen Arts Centre** has four art galleries featuring the works of Aboriginal artists of the Central Desert region. Also here is the **Museum of Central Australia**, devoted to Central Australia's natural history, and the **Strehlow Centre**, displaying Aboriginal artefacts collected from the early to mid-20th century by anthropologist T.G.H. Strehlow, who became a researcher among the Arrernte people, winning their trust.

Located 3km (2 miles) out of town along Larapinta Drive is the **Alice Springs Desert Park** (open daily 7.30am–6pm; <www.alicespringsdesertpark.com.au>; admission fee), renowned for its achievements in breeding rare and endangered species. A visit starts with a 20-minute film, then you tour

Aboriginal land

The Aboriginal Land Act of 1976 returned about one-third of the Northern Territory to Aboriginal ownership. You need a permit to enter many Aborigine-controlled areas, but not to drive through them on a public road.

Entering the home straight at the Imparja Camel Cup

walk-through enclosures and see the desert animals, which include emus, red kangaroos, reptiles and birds of prey.

Five kilometres (3 miles) east of The Alice on the Ross Highway, the **Frontier Camel Farm** (tel: 1800 806 499) offers camel rides. In mid-July each year, the local Lions Club sponsors the **Imparja Camel Cup** – an exciting day of camel races at Blatherskite Park. The animals are launched from a kneeling start in a cloud of dust, and run just as fast as race-horses, though rather less gracefully.

A popular excursion from The Alice concentrates on **Standley Chasm**, 50km (30 miles) to the west. This passage through the MacDonnell Ranges dwindles to the narrowest gap. The walls are so high and steep that the sun penetrates the bottom only fleetingly at midday. A few slender trees sprout from the rockface high above, reflected in the cool, still water of a natural pool at the far end of the gorge. In the wet season, from November to March, rain can suddenly flood the chasm.

A tourist drive called **The Red Centre Way** gives an incredible Outback experience. From Alice Springs, it heads through the western MacDonnell Ranges to Hermannsburg, a former Aboriginal mission, to **Kings Canyon** (in Watarrka National Park), and then on through the desert to **Yulara**, the site of Uluru (Ayers Rock). The trip covers about 1,200km (750 miles) and takes between three and five days. Much of the route is unsealed, so you will need a four-wheel drive vehicle. You will also need a permit to travel through Aboriginal land (for permits and information, contact the Alice Springs Visitor Information Centre, tel: 1800 645 199).

Uluru (Ayers Rock)

As the sun begins to set, crowds with their cameras gather by car and bus along 'Sunset Strip', the tongue-in-cheek name for a dusty stretch of car park. As the onlookers watch **Uluru (Ayers Rock)** (entrance fee for a 3-day pass) undergo its striking changes of colour, the mood is festive, friendly and relaxed. By coming here, visitors are fulfilling an Australian dream, getting to know this mystical 500-million-year-old rock that rises up from the red heart of the country.

The world's greatest rock, seemingly dropped by divine design in the middle of nowhere, actually protrudes from a buried mountain range. At 348m (1,142ft) tall and some 8km (5 miles) around, it is even more impressive than the dimensions suggest. Standing alone in a landscape as flat as a floor, and tinted as bright as in your imagination, the monolith certainly lives up to its reputation. It's not hard to understand why the Aborigines consider it sacred.

For the Aborigines it's not just a rock, it's a vital aspect of Dreamtime, encompassing the creation of the earth, linked with the life of the present and future. Aboriginal people have owned the rock under Australian law only since 1985. The

Uluru (Ayers Rock) is the tip
of a buried mountain range

local Anangu community leases it
back to the government for use as
a national park in return for a
healthy income and participation
in its management, but there is a
caveat: tourists may climb over the
rock on a defined path, but the sacred places (signposted) are still out
of bounds.

The most inspiring views of the
rock are to be seen at dawn and
dusk. It's well worth getting up at
6am to stake out the mighty silhouette from 20km (12 miles) away,
waiting for the sunrise. As first
light strikes the lonely monolith it
appears to catch fire, glowing red,
then orange, finally seeming to
emit rays of wondrous power. Only
then the desert world comes to life: a hawk squawks, a rabbit rustles the brush, and hordes of pesky flies begin to buzz.
(Waving your hand in front of your face soon becomes second nature in the Outback. Insect repellent helps, too, but
the flies seem to outnumber the people 20 to one.)

If you're fit you can join the crowds climbing the rock,
although local Anangu Aboriginal people regard this as dis-
respectful. A few hours are enough for the return trip via the
marked trail, which has a protective chain you can grab
when the going gets too steep or windy. The ascent requires
no mountain-climbing experience or equipment, but do wear
sensible rubber-soled shoes and carry drinking water. From

ground-level the climbers reaching the summit look like a line of very tired ants. Some climbers have died during the experience; they are commemorated by plaques placed discreetly on the base of the rock. The plaques reveal causes of death to be generally heart attacks among older climbers and fatal plunges by younger ones. The park authorities ask visitors not to climb if the temperature is over 36°C (97°F), if the track is wet, or if rain is forecast.

Another worthwhile (and safer) way to get to know the rock is to circumnavigate the base on foot, either on your own (you won't get lost) or on a ranger-guided tour. Up close, the monolith discloses its variegated surface, with its

The red road to Kata Tjuta: the name means 'many heads'

caves, dry rivulets, furrows, wounds and gashes, and what might be taken for fanciful engravings 60m (200ft) tall. Alternatively you can take a 30-minute scenic flight from Yulara or a day-trip by air from Alice Springs to get a bird's eye view of the rock and its surroundings.

Only 36km (22 miles) by road west of Ayers Rock, and visible from its summit, is another stupendous rock formation, **Kata Tjuta (The Olgas)**. From afar, Mt Olga and its satellites look like a scattering of dinosaur eggs or sleeping elephants, but they're even higher than Ayers Rock. Here, too, dawn and dusk colour the most fascinating views, the fantasy shapes changing with the hues and the movement of the shadows. You can get to know the Olgas by a choice of hiking routes. The popular trail from the Kata Tjuta car park up to the lookout is officially called 'suitable for family enjoyment', but it's steep and tricky enough to deter both the very youngest and oldest generations.

The Yulara Development

To cope with hundreds of thousands of visitors each year at Ayers Rock, a comprehensive resort has been built. It could have been a disastrous blot on the landscape, but the **Ayers Rock Resort (Yulara)** fits in benignly, 20km (12 miles) from the rock. The complex is almost entirely camouflaged, and too low-slung to detract from the majesty of the surroundings.

The facilities range from tents and caravans to a five-star hotel with gardens, pool, spa, restaurants and bars and, of course, air-conditioning. The visitors' centre in the complex offers information, literature and audio-visual shows explaining the desert, the wildlife, geology, mythology and other angles to enhance your appreciation of the Red Centre.

Several airlines serve Yulara, and the views of the desert on the way are spellbinding. Otherwise you can take a bus or drive; it's about 450km (280 miles) by paved road from Alice Springs, a whole day in which to become acquainted with the desert in its many forms – flat and desolate or covered with scrub, thinly forested or, more rarely, sand undulating in postcard-worthy dunes.

The best time of year to visit is between May and October, when the days are sunny and warm and the nights refreshingly chill. In January, by contrast, the mean maximum temperature is 36.6°C (98°F) – not quite conducive to hiking.

Surviving the Outback

Three-quarters of Australian land is desert – 'burning wastes of barren soil and sand', as the poet Henry Lawson described it. These vast empty spaces on the map hold an irresistible challenge for intrepid adventurers. Only vaguely comparable with desert of the Sahara type, the far Outback supports vegetation – sometimes even luxuriant – and fascinating wildlife. If you do want to venture off the surfaced roads and explore the unknown, there are a few precautions you must take.

• Do not even consider driving into the Outback in the summer; the heat is unbearable. In the 1840s, explorer Charles Sturt recorded temperatures of 69°C (157°F) in the open and 56°C (132°F) in the shade.

• Rain can also be a source of disaster; after many years of drought, it can suddenly pour down for an entire week, and the land is transformed into an enormous flood plain. So make sure you never camp in a dry riverbed.

• Your vehicle should be a reliable four-wheel-drive, with a complete set of spare parts: two spare tyres and tyre repair kit, two spare tubes, coil, condenser, fan belt, radiator hoses and distributor points, a tin of radiator leak fixative, spark plugs, an extra jack (with a large baseplate to prevent sinking in sand or mud), 5 litres (a gallon) of engine oil, a pump, a tool-kit, an axe and a small shovel. Keep the petrol tank full and carry at least 20 litres (5 gal) in reserve.

• You will need reliable maps and be sure to plan your route in detail – and stick to the plan relentlessly. At your point of departure, advise the police of your route, the estimated time of arrival at your destination, and the amount of rations you are carrying. Report to the police again when you arrive. Always seek local advice about the hazards you may encounter. If you wish to enter Aboriginal lands, you must first obtain permission from the Aboriginal landowners, and at least four weeks' notice is required. Inquire at the government tourist office for the appropriate address *(see page 250)*. In some areas you have to be equipped with a two-way radio.

• Take adequate supplies. Most important is water – you will need 6 litres (1½ gal) per person per day, best carried in metal containers. Emergency rations should be made up of high-energy foods such as dried fruit, with canned meats, soup and fruit drinks. Some invaluable components of your first-aid kit will be aspirin, water-purifying tablets, salt tablets, diarrhoea pills, insect repellent, disinfectant, bandages and sun-block. Your personal survival kit, which you should carry with you at all times, must contain a compass, map, whistle, waterproof matches, pocket knife, bandage and adhesive plaster.

- Other essentials: a set of billycans (pails or pots with lids and wire bails), several sheets of heavy-duty plastic (2m/6ft square) and a length of rubber or plastic tubing. A piece of nylon rope (30m/100ft long) may also come in handy.

- Wear loose, light cotton clothing and cover your head. Space blankets can prove a boon: the shiny aluminium side turned towards the sun

Water is scarce in the Outback

reflects heat away from the body, keeping the temperature normal. To keep warm, turn the shiny side inwards.

- Do not drive at night. Kangaroos are a real hazard, and you may collide with wild water buffalo, attracted to the roads at night because the surface is warmer than the ground itself.

In Case of Catastrophe

If your car breaks down, above all do not panic. *Stay with your vehicle*; it will be a welcome source of shade, and it is more easily spotted by aircraft than a person on their own. Do not risk searching for help during the day or night.

- Make visible distress signals, using brightly coloured clothing or anything that contrasts with the earth.

• Move around as little as possible, to conserve your body fluid. All your physical exertion should take place during the cool night hours.

• Your main preoccupation must be water. It is important to ration your supply and set about collecting more by making a solar still, as follows: dig a hole about 1m (3ft) square and 50cm (20in) deep, away from shade. Place a large billy-can (pail or pot) in the bottom of the hole, and surround it with leafy foliage. Then cover the hole with a sheet of plastic and seal the edges completely with earth, making sure that the plastic does not touch the interior walls of the hole. If you have a length of rubber or plastic tubing, place it in the bottom of the billycan before you seal the edges of the sheeting, leaving the other end outside to act as a siphon. Place a small stone in the centre of the plastic sheet, right over the billycan. Moisture from the ground will condense on the underside of the plastic sheet and will drip slowly into the billycan. In this way you will collect about 2 litres (½ gal) of water per hole per day, so it's best to make several stills, at least 3m (about 10ft) apart. You will need to change the position of the still every three to four days.

• Small animals – frogs, lizards and snakes – are attracted to the stills and may provide an extra source of food. In principle, anything that walks, crawls, swims, flies or grows from the soil is edible – or so they say. But beware of anything that has a bitter taste and of plants with a milky sap.

• Another source of food and water in the northwest of Australia is the bottle-tree, which preserves water in its hollow trunk for months after the wet season has ended. In an emergency you can also eat the rind of bottle-tree pods, chopped up and stirred with water.

The prospects may seem harrowing, but after all, the Aboriginals have survived and even thrived in this forbidding land for at least 50,000 years.

Western Australia has plenty of elbow room

WESTERN AUSTRALIA

When it comes to elbow room, the state of Western Australia has no competition. It's bigger than Texas and Alaska combined and more than 10 times the area of Great Britain.

Most of the state's vast expanse is desert, semi-desert or otherwise difficult terrain. The bulk of the population of 2 million has therefore gravitated to the Mediterranean climate found around the beautiful capital city of Perth. Closer to Jakarta than to Sydney, Perth faces the Indian Ocean with an open, outward-looking stance. Here the cares of the big population centres of eastern Australia seem worlds away.

The state's Outback produces great wealth, and even the forbidding deserts are bursting with minerals. It was gold that brought the state's first bonanza, during the 1880s and 1890s, followed by nickel, bauxite and iron. Considerably more appealing are the above-ground riches: the hardwood forests, the orchards, the vineyards and the springtime wild flowers. And, since the climate is so sunny, it's only fair that there is a beach for every possible mood along the 6,400km (4,000 miles) of coastline.

The first European to set eyes on a Western Australian beach (in 1616) was Dirk Hartog, a Dutch navigator making his way from the Cape of Good Hope to Java. It was not long before other Dutch travellers touched base here, and one of them reported spotting a wallaby, though not by name; he thought it was a giant cat with a pouch for its kitten. Later in the 17th century, the British adventurer William Dampier happened upon Shark Bay, near Carnarvon, and could hardly wait to leave: the land seemed hopeless for farming, there was no drinking water, and he dismissed the indigenous population as 'brutes'.

More than 200 years after Hartog's discovery of Western Australia, the British finally got around to colonising it. The site chosen, on the Swan River, became Perth. But what the Colonial Office considered a good idea turned out to be less

From Coast to Coast

It takes just 4½ hours to fly from the South Pacific to the Indian Ocean, from Sydney to Perth, but if you have 68 hours to spare, you can make the journey by train. The Indian-Pacific, a luxurious but not particularly rapid train operated by Great Southern Railways (<www.gsr.com.au>), crosses the country twice a week in each direction. On its 4,352-km (2,702-mile) journey, it crosses the Nullarbor Plain, with one section that's the world's longest stretch of straight track – 479km (298 miles) without a bend. There are numerous stops, but few towns, and none of any importance. In fact, there's not much to see – nothing but scrub, blue sky and telegraph poles for days on end – but passengers are well catered for with an observation lounge, a bar and even a music room.

brilliant in practice. It would take more than the scenery and the climate to attract settlers to what seemed, even by Australian standards, the end of the world. Problems of development persisted, including poor communications, financial difficulties and a shortage of workers. Prospects for the new frontier became so precarious that the colony's leaders had to make an

Black swans are as noisy as they are handsome

appeal to London, asking the government to send over a supply of forced labourers – convicts.

Even so, nothing really worked in Western Australia until the gold rush during the 1890s, when the population quadrupled in just 10 years. Throughout the 20th century and up to the present, the exploitation of mineral deposits throughout the state provided the main basis of its wealth – from uranium and iron ore to gas and oil. Once it was launched on the road to prosperity, there was no stopping Australia's largest state. Its isolation finally ended in the early years of the 20th century, when the transcontinental railway linked Perth and Sydney.

Perth

Bright new high-rise office buildings scrape the clear blue skies of **Perth**. If this city brimming with vigour and enthusiasm were a person, you might imagine it had been born with the proverbial silver spoon in its mouth: a handsome, clean-cut youngster with every possible advantage, inevitably growing up to become an unqualified success in life.

Although history refutes the silver-spoon theory, you can't miss Perth's easy self-confidence. The people are relaxed, friendly and anxious to help the stranger. They are proud of their efficient town and its up-to-date facilities – the stylish shopping arcades, the art galleries and Entertainment Centre – and the great sailing, swimming, surfing and fishing right on its doorstep. The inhabitants won't fail to inform you that this tidy city sprawling magnificently along the looping river is Australia's sunniest state capital.

Sunshine aside, Perth has called itself 'the city of lights' since the early days of the American manned space programme. As John Glenn, the first American to orbit the earth, passed over the city, middle-of-the-night Perth switched on every light bulb in town. It was a friendly gesture that brightened the lone astronaut's flight and put Perth's name in lights.

Perth's skyscrapers are crowded around the Swan River

City Sights

Few will get a chance to enjoy a spaceman's perspective, but the view over Perth from **King's Park** is a good compromise for sizing up the city below. These 400 hectares (990 acres) of natural woodland and wild flowers, manicured lawns and picnic sites, solemn monuments, bike tracks and lively play-grounds are found on the top of a bluff called **Mt Eliza**, right on the edge of the city centre. From here you look down on the wide Swan River as it meanders toward the sea, on the business district with its gleaming skyscrapers, and on the complexity of the well-landscaped municipal freeway system.

The **Swan River** was named after the indigenous black swans found here, first noted with amazement by the 17th-century Dutch navigator Willem de Vlaming. Unlike swans in the Northern Hemisphere, which are white and prone to whistling or grunting when they are not naturally mute, the black swans sound off like a band of clarinets noisily tuning up. They're such tame creatures that they'll take bread out of the palm of your hand without biting.

The Swan River begins about 240km (150 miles) inland in the wheatlands of Western Australia. For most of its long journey, under the name of Avon River, it is only seasonally navigable. But here, with the Indian Ocean close enough to salt it, the Swan widens into a lake, and invites reflection – and attracts flotillas of yachts. By the riverside in the centre of town, the **Old Courthouse** really is old, especially by local standards. Built in Georgian style in 1836, it's the old-est public building in Perth and houses the Francis Burt law museum (open Mon, Tues and Fri 10am–2.30pm).

Stirling Gardens, surrounding the courthouse, is a rest-ful hideaway. The 'Ore Obelisk' monument here looks like a giant shish-kebab impaling all of the minerals mined in Western Australia; but don't expect to find gold or diamonds on the skewer – they don't seem to count.

View from Swan Bells Tower

Nearby, fronting the river, the Barrack Street Jetty, where ferries leave for Rottnest Island, is the site of the striking steel, glass and copper **Swan Bells Tower** (open daily 10am–4pm; admission fee), completed in 2001. The 82.5-m (270-ft) spire houses the 14th-century bells of the church of St-Martin-in-the-Fields, London – a Bicentennial present from Queen Elizabeth II – which ring out every day, except Wed and Fri, at noon–1pm. A top-floor observation deck gives views of the Perth skyline.

The **Town Hall**, at the corner of Hay and Barrack Streets, was built in the 1860s by convicts. If you look closely at the outline of the windows of the tower, you may perceive the design of broad arrows – the prison symbol that was stencilled on convict uniforms. Similarly Tudor in inspiration, but even less of an antique than the Town Hall, **London Court** is a 1930s shopping mall done up in 16th-century style. It fits in quite happily with the modern stores and interconnecting shopping precincts radiating from the **Hay Street Mall**, Perth's main shopping street. Cars are prohibited here, so the window-shopping is very relaxed.

A couple of blocks north, across Murray Street Mall, is **Forrest Place** on the corner of Wellington Street. Here, in Albert Facey House, you'll find the Western Australian Visitor Centre (tel: 1800 812 808).

In a city as young as Perth, with its skyline of tall, modern office buildings, those historic structures which have escaped the developer's demolition ball are proudly pointed out to visitors. **Government House**, on the main street, St George's Terrace, is the official residence of the Western Australia governor. Its Gothic effects date from the 1860s. Built by hard-working convicts, the house is used nowadays for state occasions and to accommodate visiting VIPs.

The elegant terrace leads directly to the **Barracks Archway**, the last vestige of a headquarters building of the 1860s. This crenellated three-storey structure has been preserved as a memorial to the early colonists. Behind the brick archway you can glimpse **Parliament House**, where the state legislature sits.

On the other side of the railway tracks – you can cross the unusual Horseshoe Bridge by foot or car – stands the **Perth Cultural Centre**, which is made up of Western Australia's state museum and art gallery, state library and the **Perth Institute of Contemporary Arts** (PICA; open Tues–Sun 11am–6pm, Fri till 9pm; free). Part of the **Western Australian Museum** (open daily 9.30am–5pm; <www.museum.wa.gov.au>; free) is the **Old Gaol**, which was constructed and used by convicts in 1856. The museum offers more than penal relics – there is also an extensive collection of Aboriginal rock paintings, head-dresses and weapons, and a 10-tonne meteorite. The **Art Gallery of Western Australia** (open daily 10am–5pm; <www.artgallery.wa.gov.au>; free) displays paintings from several continents.

Also north of the city centre is the **Northbridge**

Statue at the Cultural Centre

district, which is full of lively ethnic restaurants, pubs and nightclubs, especially around James and Lake streets. If you're in the mood for gambling, head for the **Burswood Entertainment Complex**, near the Causeway Bridge. Here, under one roof, you'll find a casino, a nightclub, restaurants, bars, and Perth's two main entertainment venues, a 2,300-seater theatre and the 20,000-seater **Burswood Dome**, which can pack them in for rock concerts, ballet, sporting and other events.

In the centre of town is the Concert Hall, the headquarters of the state's symphony orchestra. If you're looking for stage plays, the most atmospheric house is **His Majesty's Theatre**, a plush Edwardian pile.

North of the centre, the **Aquarium of Western Australia** (open daily 10am–5pm; <www.aqwa.com.au>; admission fee), an underwater-tunnel aquarium with interactive displays, offers whale-watching trips in season. For action entertainment, try the thrill rides at **Adventure World Theme Park** (open outside school holidays, Thur–Mon 10am–5pm; school holidays, daily; admission fee), 15km (9 miles) south of the city. Nearby, you can try bungee-jumping from a 40-m (131-ft) tower at **Bungee West** (bookings, tel: (08) 9417 2500), or parasail to see the sights of the city from a higher perspective.

To the Coast

It's only 19km (12 miles) down the river from Perth to the capital's Indian Ocean port, Fremantle – an enjoyable outing on one of the cruise boats that ply the Swan River. The river tours begin in the centre of Perth, at the **Barrack Street Jetty**. On the south side of the **Narrows Bridge**, note the **Old Mill**, built in 1835, an imposing white windmill in the Dutch style from the first half of the 19th century. Perfectly restored, it's open for visits (Tues–Sun 10am–4pm).

Beyond this, on the opposite shore, just past Kings Park, spreads what looks like another transplant from Europe. The campus of the **University of Western Australia** was constructed and landscaped in a Mediterranean style, from the shrubs right up to the orange-tiled roofs. **Matilda Bay** harbours only a relative handful of the swarms of sailing boats that call the Swan River home. During World War II this was a base for Catalina flying boats. The bay is now the site of the Royal Perth Yacht Club.

The coastline of the Dalkeith district, near **Point Resolution**, is called Millionaires' Row. The view of these fine mansions from the perspective of the river might evoke a dash of envy;

Open-air concert, Matilda Bay

even millionaires from out of town could become jealous at the sheer opulence of these homes.

Freshwater Bay was named by the crew of HMS *Beagle*, the survey ship made famous as the vehicle for Charles Darwin's researches into natural selection. Beyond this bay, and a zigzag, the river tapers to a fairly narrow-gauge artery spanned by two bridges. Long-suffering convict labour built the first bridge at this site in 1866. It proved a boon to one of its creators, a celebrated outlaw named Moondyne Joe, an escape artist. The night before the ribbon-cutting ceremony, he broke out of Fremantle Prison and gave himself the honour of becoming the first, if unofficial, pedestrian to cross the bridge over the Swan River. He made a clean getaway.

Fremantle

Colonial architecture, Fremantle

Although it's a serious international port, you'll remember the city of Fremantle for its casual charms. The town's special character combines a Mediterranean-style sunniness with a lovely Victorian quaintness. Although the town is pretty cosmopolitan, it is also as down-to-earth as its classic examples of convict architecture.

For many years Fremantle – 'Freo' to the Aussies – lay becalmed, a long way from the big time of tourism. Then came the America's Cup saga and a sudden saturation of world attention. New-found pride inspired the townsfolk in their sparkling campaign to restore the old terraced houses and other relics in time for the 1986–87 defence of the Cup. The marina facilities were also expanded and improved.

Whether you think of Fremantle as a yachting base or a workaday port, you'll want to see the sights of the harbour. There is a mixture of dream yachts, trawlers, ocean liners and cargo ships of every stripe.

Fremantle's highest point is **Monument Hill** in **War Memorial Park**. There are three memorials altogether, including one for the US personnel based in Fremantle who died in World War II. Another, an original periscope, commemorates the British and Allied submarine crews who perished in the same conflict. This is the place to watch the sun set over the Indian Ocean.

Back near the waterfront, and wasting an enviable view, the 12-sided **Round House** (open daily 10.30am–3.30pm; free) looks like the forbidding, windowless prison it used to be. Actually it's much more cheerful from the inside, with its sunny courtyard. Constructed in 1831, the Round House specialised in the lesser criminals, although it was the site of the state's first hanging; generally, incorrigibles were shipped off to the rigours of Tasmania.

But the more compelling penal complex is the **Old Fremantle Prison** (open daily 10am–5pm for guided tours only), convict-built in 1855 and continuously in operation as a maximum security prison until the early 1990s. Since 1992 it has been one of Fremantle's most popular attractions; the fascinating guided tours leave every 30 minutes, and after-dark candlelit tours are also offered (bookings, tel: (08) 9336 9200).

In pride of place on Victoria Quay is the **Western Australian Maritime Museum** (open daily 9.30am–5pm; <www.museum.gov.au/maritime>; admission fee), which highlights the state's maritime heritage. The **Shipwreck Gallery** (open daily 9.30am–5pm; free) is housed separately, in the convict-built Commissariat on Cliff Street. Here's a chance to see some notable wrecks such as the wooden hull of the *Batavia*, the flagship of the Dutch East India Company, which went aground in 1629 and was salvaged and restored in the late 20th century.

The **Fremantle Arts Centre** (open daily 10am–5pm;

In the Maritime Museum

free), at the other end of town, houses a gallery of contemporary art in a converted Victorian lunatic asylum.

If you're visiting Fremantle at the weekend, check out the lively **markets** on the corner of Henderson Street and South Terrace (Fri 9am–9pm, Sat 9am–5pm, Sun 10am–5pm).

Rottnest Island

Don't be put off by the name: there is nothing rotten in the state of Western Australia, and certainly not on Rottnest Island (<www.rottnestisland.com>). Even in the original Dutch, the name does the island no justice. Apparently Commodore Willem de Vlaming, who landed here in 1696, confused the indigenous quokkas (a species of small wallaby) with some imaginary species of rat. So he called the island Rottnest, or rat's nest. In spite of this unkind mistake, the Dutch explorer considered Rottnest an earthly paradise. You may well agree.

Befriending a quokka

A good reason for going over the sea to Rottnest (18km/11 miles from Fremantle) is to see the fetching little quokkas, with babies in their pouches, like their kangaroo cousins. Other attractions are peacocks and pheasants, which were introduced when the governors of Western Australia used the island as a summer residence. And you can spot dozens of other species of birds, including the osprey. Since 1941 the island has been a wildlife sanctuary, where it's forbidden to tamper with any of nature, even the snakes.

Rottnest is as quiet as an idyllic, barefoot sort of isle ought to be. The number of cars is severely limited. Bikes are the most popular way of exploring the 40km (25 miles) of coastline. Look into the swimming, snorkelling, fishing and boating opportunities.

Three ferry operators serve Rottnest Island (nicknamed 'Rotto' by Aussies) from Perth or Fremantle. It's a 30-minute cruise from Fremantle and about double that from Perth. You can fly there in 20 minutes.

Excursions Inland

Just to the east of Perth, the **Darling Range** is the beginning of a great inland plateau. Amid the tall trees and colourful wild flowers are lookout points with superb views of the city and the sea. Waterfalls, brooks and dams refresh the relaxing scene.

The **Swan Valley**, only about half an hour's drive northeast of Perth, is a high-priority destination for wine-lovers. The area is noted for its small, family-run vineyards. The wine-making tradition in the Swan Valley dates back to the foundation of Western Australia. If wine-tasting and driving seem incompatible, you can take a coach tour of selected vineyards, or the even more popular river cruise with stops at one or two wine-cellars.

Further east, the 150-km (90-mile) green expanse of the **Avon Valley** provides pastureland for cattle and grows the grain to feed Perth and beyond. The colony's first inland settlement, **York** is proud of its history. More than a dozen 19th-century buildings, including an extravagantly designed Town Hall, have been restored; several now serve as museums. Just outside town, one of the early farms has been restored to a 'living museum' in which you can watch blacksmiths and wheelwrights at work. Clydesdale horses still plough the fields.

Yanchep National Park, 50km (30 miles) to the north of Perth, is known for its eucalyptus forests, wild flowers (in bloom in September) and a series of limestone caves. There is also an island-studded lake called **Loch McNess**, named after a local philanthropist, Sir Charles McNess. Don't bother looking for a Loch McNess monster. You can, however, see a koala colony here.

For those interested in wild flowers, the coastal town of **Geraldton**, 420km (260 miles) north of Perth, makes a good base for exploring the surrounding areas, such as Kalbarri National Park, where the flowers are at their best in August.

Natural Wonders

A spectacle reckoned to be more than 2.5 billion years old is **Wave Rock** – one of those natural phenomena worth a long detour. And it will probably require one – it's a 700-km (437-mile) round trip by road from Perth. The rock stands near the small town of **Hyden**, about 350km (220 miles) inland from Perth, in the wide-open spaces where the wheat, oats and barley grow. The rock itself takes the form of a stupendous surfer's wave, as tall as a five-storey building, eternally on the verge of breaking. Walking under the impending splash is one of the state's most popular tourist activities. Energetic visitors can also climb to the top. Other extraordinary rock formations in the area have expressive names like Hippo's Yawn and The Humps.

In **Nambung National Park**, about 250km (155 miles) north of Perth, the **Pinnacles Desert** is notable for myriad limestone pillars jutting like stalagmites from the desert floor. Standing as high as 5–6m (16–20ft), the Pinnacles are scattered over perhaps 400 hectares (1,000 acres). The imagination runs wild. When Dutch explorers first sighted the Pinnacles from their vessels in the 17th century, they thought they had found the ruins of a long-deserted city. In fact, they are entirely natural. Limestone formed around the roots of plants growing on stable dunes about 30,000 years ago. The plants died and the dunes moved on, leaving the calcified structures exposed. The park's

Exploring the Pinnacles Desert

entrance is located near the fishing village of Cervantes.

The Southwest

Excursions to the southwestern corner of the state encompass a delightful variety of scenery: beaches, vineyards, orchards, wild flowers (September is best) and forests of jarrah, karri and marri, eucalyptus species not found anywhere else. You can see some of these majestic trees – up to 70m (230ft) high – in **Leeuwin-Naturaliste National Park**, just west of Margaret River (see page 138), and near **Pemberton**, 140km (90 miles) south of Margaret River.

Bunbury is a pleasant vacation town in the southwest, 180km (110 miles) from Perth, and you can swim with the

The Margaret River region has some of Australia's best surf

amazingly tame dolphins at Koombana beach there. The **Margaret River** region, between Cape Naturaliste and Cape Leeuwin, is honeycombed with limestone caves, some of which are open to the public. Near Yallingup, **Ngilgi Caves** (open daily 9.30am–3.30pm; tel: (08) 9755 2152) form a fantastic underground world of elaborately carved limestone.

Margaret River lies at the heart of the state's top wine-growing and gourmet dining region. Specialities include brie, fresh berries and marron (freshwater shellfish), while accommodation ranges from boutique guest-houses to five-star hotels or campsites. Places to stay include Cape Lodge, built in South African Cape style. Margaret River township is the perfect spot from which to tour the region's noted vineyards, including Vasse Felix, Clairault, Sandalford, Leeuwin Estate, Xanadu and Cape Mentelle. This area is also famed as one of the nation's best surfing locations. The closest beaches are at Prevelly, 10 minutes' drive from town.

The Goldfields

Kalgoorlie, located around 550km (340 miles) east of Perth, retains the atmosphere of the riotous gold-rush town it was in the 1890s. The streets, laid out in a grid, are wide enough for stagecoaches or camel trains to make a U-turn. It's like a Wild West movie set, and there are verandahed saloons for every occasion. Optimists still scan old worked-over sites in search of forgotten nuggets – the occasional whopper still turns up.

The first big strike of Kalgoorlie gold came in June 1893, when an Irishman named Patrick Hannan stumbled onto enough glitter to really kick up a fuss. A bronze statue of the bearded prospector has a place of honour in Kalgoorlie's main street, which bears his name.

When Hannan's news spread, the almost total lack of water was the first desperate hardship to face the thousands of prospectors who rushed headlong into the goldfields. Disease and death from dehydration took a heavy toll. The solution was found by another Irishman, an engineer named C.Y. O'Connor who constructed a 560-km (350-mile) pipeline from a reservoir near Perth. You can still see the big above-ground pipes by the side of the road. Wounded by criticism of the project, O'Connor killed himself before the first drop of water reached Kalgoorlie; he is now honoured by a statue on the waterfront in Fremantle.

As the prospectors came in from the surrounding desert with their sudden wealth, Kalgoorlie – and its neighbouring twin town of Boulder – turned into a rip-roaring supplier of wine, women and song. The pubs were legion; many still retain their frontier atmosphere. Another old mining tradition is the red-light district of Hay Street, although at last inspection only three of the notorious 'tin-shack' brothels were still in business. You can gauge how prosperous the town was from the elegance of the Victorian buildings, most notably in the three-storey **Western Australia Museum,**

Kalgoorlie-Boulder (open daily 10am–4.30pm; free). This institution is stacked with exhibits detailing the life and work of those early prospectors.

Five kilometres (3 miles) north of Kalgoorlie along the Goldfields Highway on the site of a disused mine is the **Australian Prospectors and Miners Hall of Fame** (daily 9am–4.30pm; admission fee), which highlights Australia's mining industry. There are gold panning demonstrations, and underground tours are conducted by former miners.

A year before Paddy Hannan's big strike at Kalgoorlie, gold was discovered at **Coolgardie**, 40km (25 miles) to the west. Today Coolgardie proudly bears the slogan of 'ghost town'. In fact, ghosting is its principal industry, and if there's a bit of melancholy in the air, it can only be good for business. The historical markers here seem to far outnumber the population, which at the turn of the 20th century was 15,000 and now stands at about 800. Any good ghost town needs an interesting cemetery, and the inscriptions on the headstones in Coolgardie's graveyard tell revealing stories of the harsh frontier life. Among the Afghan camel drivers buried here, at least one is listed as having been murdered.

Wet and dry

Like all of Australia's tropical north, the Kimberley has two seasons: the dry (April to October) and the wet (November to March). Avoid the wet season. Not only is the humidity very high at this time, but the often torrential rainfall can rapidly turn rivers from mere trickles into raging torrents, flooding vast tracts of land. Many minor roads are closed for the entire wet season.

The Kimberley

More than 1,500km (930 miles) north of the gold lode, one of the richest diamond mines in the world gives a sparkle to the rugged and remote **Kimberley** region of Western Australia.

Driving through the Kimberley

The **Argyle mine** produces a sizeable heap of exquisite pink diamonds – a coveted rarity in the gem world – as well as vast quantities of industrial diamonds that are used for grinding and drilling. Machines beside which humans look like Lilliputians move the ore along to the Argyle processing plant, where millions of glittering carats are then yielded per year.

The Kimberley, a dramatic, elemental and spectacular area of waterfalls, thunderstorms, searing heat and torrential rain (the latter two depending on season), is thought to hide as many as half of all the diamonds on earth. But that's not its only distinction.

More than three times the size of England, the Kimberley has fewer people per square kilometre than almost anywhere else in the world. Generations of isolation have left the Kimberley the most Aboriginal part of Australia. Some 30 percent of land is Aboriginal-owned and nearly half the population of 29,000 is black.

The extraordinary Bungle Bungles in Purnululu National Park

The enormous region is particularly known for Aboriginal rock art, including the mysterious '**Bradshaw figures**', named after explorer Joseph Bradshaw, the first European to describe them. In 1891, Bradshaw wrote: 'The most remarkable fact in connection with these drawings is that wherever a profile face is shown, the features are of a most pronounced aquiline type, quite different from those of any native we encountered. Indeed, looking at some of the groups, one might almost think himself viewing the painted walls of an Egyptian temple.' The drawings are believed by scholars to have derived from an unknown culture that flourished some time before 15,000BC – long before the Egyptians had built their temples.

Until a few decades ago, the Kimberley was the domain of intrepid explorers. It has been opened up since, with tour operators using four-wheel-drive vehicles, boats, helicopters and small aircraft to reach the region's far-flung attractions:

towering gorges on the Fitzroy River; **Purnululu (Bungle Bungle) National Park** with its orange-and-black beehive-striped mounds; the sandstone and volcanic country of **Prince Regent Nature Reserve**; the stunning gorge on the Fitzroy River of the **Geikie Gorge National Park**; the tidal 'waterfalls' near Derby; and the eerie **Wolfe Creek Meteorite National Park**. The crater was formed 300,000 years ago and is 850m (930yds) across, with a rim 50m (165ft) high. Aborigines call the area *Kandimalal*, which means 'the place where the snake emerged from the ground'. Europeans only discovered it in 1947. It was the setting of an Australian horror movie, *Wolf Creek*, in 2005.

Coastal Attractions

On the coast, the seaport of **Broome** has a romantic past. It once supplied 80 percent of all the world's mother-of-pearl. Divers from Japan, Malaya and the Philippines went out on 400 boats, diving for oysters and the pearls within them. The Asian aura still lingers, even though the mother-of-pearl business died with the introduction of cultured pearls and plastic buttons. You will find evidence of past glories in **Chinatown**, in the old Japanese boarding houses, and in the gambling and other pleasure palaces – all reminders of the port's early 20th-century heyday.

The main attraction today is **Cable Beach**, a fantastic 22-km (14-mile) stretch of golden sands, so named when the underwater communication link between Broome and Java (and so on to London) was established in the 19th century. At **Gantheaume Point**, low tide exposes dinosaur footprints about 130 million years old. If you stay late on the beach in March–April or August–September you may be lucky enough to see a natural phenomenon called 'the Staircase to the Moon', an illusion caused by the full moon reflecting on mud flats. It can be seen from the jetty at extreme low tides.

South Australia's mascot

SOUTH AUSTRALIA

The state's official animal symbol is the hairy-nosed wombat, but don't let that put you off. This shy native of South Australia is just as cuddly as any koala (but rather heavier); it is merely lacking the services of any public relations advisers to polish up its image.

Like the amiable wombat, South Australia is self-reliant. Everything the state needs can be found within its borders: coal from the open-cut mines of Leigh Creek, gas under the northeastern desert, grain and cattle through hundreds of kilometres of latitude, fish from the Southern Ocean, and world-renowned wines from scenic vineyards. South Australia produces more wine than any Australian state, just under half of the nation's total.

The sights of South Australia are as many and varied as its resources: with the rugged grandeur of the Flinders Ranges, the sand dunes of the north, the green banks of the Murray River, and the surf of the Great Australian Bight.

The history of South Australia is distinctive. There were no convicts; the colony was founded as a planned community run by wealthy idealists. The 'free settlers only' tag is a source of local pride. Sobriety and morality were keystones of the master plan, giving rise to a reputation for stuffy puritanism. Fortunately, the influence of the state's 'wowsers' (killjoys) has long faded. For example, Maslins Beach just outside Adelaide became Australia's first legal nudist beach *(see page 156)*.

In some social respects, South Australia has led the rest of the country. It was first to grant votes to women, first to appoint an Aboriginal governor and first to appoint a woman governor. Spread across 1 million sq km (390,000 sq miles), the state occupies one-eighth of the entire continent. But because most of the state is unendurable desert, the inhabitants number only about one-thirteenth of Australia's total population. And more than three-quarters of these may be found living contentedly in the graceful capital city.

Adelaide

Adelaide is easy to reach. Its international airport is efficient, land transport links are good and the city offers a cheerful introduction to Australia. Adelaide's sunny, dry climate beams on the city's many parks and gardens, as well as its elegant squares and broad boulevards.

With a population of over one million, Adelaide is a relatively sophisticated capital, where culture and good living are important elements of the local scene. There is a significant art gallery and the world's largest collection of Aboriginal artefacts in the South Australian Museum. The city puts

Festival Frenzy

Sydney, Melbourne and Perth may all have their arts festivals, but none compares in size, prestige or sheer excitement to Adelaide's. Few cities in the world have such an extraordinary range of performance spaces, from the gleaming white Festival Centre to the outdoor amphitheatres and intimate lofts. The 'official' festival lures the high-profile international acts, kicking off with free weekend concerts and firework displays in Rundle Park. The fringe festival, for lesser-known performers and artists, attracts literally thousands of acts from all over Australia, Europe and North America. Every spare corner of indoor space is devoted to some art exhibition, and every stretch outdoors to a site-specific installation. By any standards, it's a remarkable happening.

on a world-acclaimed international festival of the arts every other year (even-numbered years) and a fringe festival annually. You can also enjoy Womadelaide every February–March, a music festival with indigenous musicians from around the world.

Every day, the locals here pay tribute to international culinary art, dining out in hundreds of excellent restaurants. Chefs work with top quality raw material. You can see and taste it at the **Central Market** in Gouger Street – fresh produce from all parts of the state, including McLaren Vale olives, Coffin Bay oysters, Barossa mettwursts and Riverland dried fruits.

Nightlife encompasses concerts, theatres, clubs and a casino. The city has come a long way since the days when outsiders joked, 'I went to Adelaide once but it was closed.'

Adelaide was founded two generations after the settlement of Sydney, in the reign of King William IV, and named after his queen, the former Princess Adelaide of Saxe-Meiningen. Although the southern coastline had been well charted, the idea of building a city beside the Torrens River didn't catch on until the 1830s. Before the first earth was turned, the city was planned on paper, street by street and park by park. The business district covers the area of 2.6 sq km (1 sq mile). The model, with its built-in green belt, was a winner, and so it remains.

City Sights

The most stately of streets in Adelaide is **North Terrace**, which delineates the northern edge of the business district. North Terrace is lined with trees and distinguished buildings – mansions and museums, churches and memorials. Between the Terrace and the landscaped bank of the river is the **Adelaide Festival Centre**, which calls to mind Sydney's Opera House, but with angular planes in place of billowing

The white Adelaide Festival Centre stands in Elder Park

curves; Adelaide also managed to truncate Sydney's lavish price tag. The relatively budget-priced $20-million complex has a theatre for every occasion. The 2,000-seat Festival Theatre is convertible, in three hours, from an opera house to a concert hall with outstanding acoustics. A drama theatre seats 600 people, an experimental theatre 400 and an outdoor amphitheatre 1,000.

There are 90-minute backstage tours of the establishment (Tues and Thur 11am, Sat 11.30am) and a theatre museum preserves South Australia's rich history and interest in the performing arts. Outside, bold sculptures are strewn around the plaza. You can eat outdoors in the Festival Centre's bistro overlooking the river, or make your own picnic on the lawn of the surrounding **Elder Park**. Or take a sightseeing boat up the river to the **zoo** (open daily 9.30am–5pm; admission fee), where you can pet the kangaroos and admire an outstanding collection of Australian birds.

The Art Gallery of South Australia, on North Terrace

Just behind the Festival Centre, the **South Australian Parliament House** (guided tours Mon–Fri on non-sitting days 10am and 2pm) is dignified by 10 Corinthian columns and so much expensive stonework it earned the nickname of the 'marble palace'. The foundation was laid in 1881 but work continued, on and off, over the following 58 years. Just across the road is **Government House**, the official residence of the Governor of South Australia.

A startling change of pace lies next door: **Adelaide Skycity** (open Sun–Thur 10am–4am, Fri–Sat 10am–6am) is a casino in a dazzling conversion of the domed old railway station. They've created a wonderfully plush gambling den with potted palms, marble floors and mighty chandeliers, which is open to the public.

Just behind the State Library is the **Migration Museum** (open Mon–Fri 10am–5pm, Sat–Sun 1pm–5pm; free), tracing the history of immigration.

Elsewhere along North Terrace, the **University of Adelaide** is at the heart of a cluster of cultural institutions. Whale skeletons fill the show windows of the excellent **South Australian Museum** (open daily 10am–5pm; <www.samuseum.sa.gov.au>; free) as an alluring invitation. Inside is a monumental collection of Aboriginal artefacts. A large-screen video display relates the story of the Aboriginal Dreamtime hero Ngurunderi. Other countries are well represented in a comprehensive survey of ceremonial masks, shields and sculptures from South Pacific islands. And you can see a traditional trading vessel from New Guinea, which remained in service until recent times, with a bamboo deck and a sail made of bark.

The **Art Gallery of South Australia** (open daily 10am–5pm; <www.artgallery.sa.gov.au>; free), which officially opened in 1881, covers many centuries of the world's art, ranging from ancient Chinese ceramics to contemporary Australian prints, drawings, paintings and sculptures. The gallery is also home to an extensive collection of Aboriginal art.

Two more historic buildings on North Terrace are **Holy Trinity Church**, the first Anglican church built in South Australia (begun in 1838), and **Ayers House** (for opening hours tel: (08) 8224 0666; <www.ayerhouse.com>), a 45-room mansion furnished in an opulent 19th-century style. The house was owned by a local businessman and statesman, Sir Henry Ayers, after whom an admiring explorer named Ayers Rock. He was premier of South Australia seven times, and used Ayers House for state functions. Its ballroom, the hub of the Adelaide social scene, was regularly washed down with milk to make the floor fast and smooth.

To the north of Ayers House lie the **Botanic Gardens**, 20 hectares (50 acres) of lawns, trees, shrubs and lakes, with some exceptional botanical buildings as well, from the old Palm House brought from Germany in 1871 to the extraordinary Bicentennial Conservatory of 1988. The restaurant has an excellent reputation.

Parallel with North Terrace is **Rundle Mall**, an all-weather pedestrian mall, and the heart of Adelaide's shopping area. Its trademark is a sculpture comprising double-decked spheres of stainless steel reflecting the animation all around. The mall's merchants include department stores, boutiques, cafés and restaurants, all enlivened by street entertainers. The **Myer Centre** and the **Adelaide Central Plaza** are multi-storey shopping centres packed with speciality shops and the city's two department stores. Rundle Street (the eastern extension of Rundle Mall) is an arty and pleasant quarter, and contains Adelaide's two best pubs, the Exeter and the Austral. The westward extension of Rundle Mall, Hindley Street, has clubs, live entertainment, amusement arcades and strip joints.

Located on Grenfell Street is **Tandanya** (open daily 10am–5pm), an outstanding Aboriginal cultural centre offering art galleries, a workshop and performing arts. The shop there is a good place to buy authentic Aboriginal souvenirs.

North of the city centre, **Light's Vision** is not a sound-and-light show, as its name may suggest. It's a monument to the foresight of Lt-Col William Light, who was sent out in 1836 to find the ideal site for a model city, then devise the total plan for its development. Atop a pedestal on Montefiore Hill, his statue peers over the parklands, pointing at the city of Adelaide, which he created.

Nearby Places

Adelaide has an outstanding public transport system, including the highly efficient O-Bahn, a 'bullet bus' that steers itself along its own smooth roadway at speeds of up to 100kph (over 60mph). But nostalgia persists: the last surviving tramcars still clatter along between the edge of Victoria Square and the seashore at suburban **Glenelg**. This lively beach resort, from which a fishing pier forges far out to sea, was the original landing-place of the colonists who founded South Australia. A full-size replica of their vessel, a converted freighter named HMS *Buffalo*, moored nearby, is now a restaurant. Also in Glenelg is the **Rodney Fox Shark Experience** (open daily 10am–5pm; <www.rodneyfox.com.au>;

admission fee), dedicated to the great white shark. The museum contains fascinating – and frightening – exhibits, such as the great white's massive jaws. Among other beaches near Adelaide, from north to south along the Gulf of St Vincent, you will find Semaphore, Grange, Henley Beach, West Beach, Somerton, Brighton and Seacliff.

South and east of the city, the **Adelaide Hills**, the last manifestation of the Flinders Ranges, provide a backdrop of forests, orchards and vineyards. There are pleasant drives, lovely walks, fine views, and plenty of picnic possibilities. You can also

By tram to Glenelg

see wildlife at close range at the **Warrawong Sanctuary** (open daily 9am–7pm; admission fee) and **Cleland Wildlife Park** (open daily 9.30am–5pm; admission fee). The highest of the hills, Mt Lofty (770m/2,525ft) is only 15 minutes out of town by car, and there are some good bush walks.

Hahndorf, a hill village situated 30km (19 miles) southeast of Adelaide, has changed little since it was settled in 1839 by German refugees. Many of the original buildings in this oldest surviving German settlement in Australia have been restored, and various folklore events brighten the tourist calendar, especially the Founders Day Festival, a marksmanship and beer-drinking celebration every January, and St Nicholas Night in December.

Up the River

The **Murray River** begins life in the Snowy Mountains (the Australian Alps), becomes the frontier between Victoria and New South Wales, and enjoys its last meandering through the state of South Australia. It is the river that accounts for the beautiful vineyards, orchards and pastures along the way, not to mention the boating, fishing and waterskiing. In the 19th century the river was a main thoroughfare for both passengers and cargo, but the advent of railways and highways left the Murray more of a pleasure route.

Paddle steamers churn up nostalgia along the lower Murray, only an hour's drive from Adelaide. A variety of boats offer short excursions or voyages of several days. It's also possible to hire a houseboat and ply the river at your own pace, in which case you can fish for your own dinner. The Murray cod run to gargantuan sizes, and you can also catch 'yabbies', big freshwater crustaceans akin to crayfish.

The Barossa Valley

Australia's best-known wine-producing region, the **Barossa Valley**, just 50km (30 miles) northeast of Adelaide, is also one of the prettiest. The scenery is beautiful: soft hills, sheep-grazing land, cosy villages, and the rows of vines that produce some famous wines – the 50 or so wineries produce about a quarter of Australia's total vintage. The valley is easy to explore: just 30km (19 miles) long by 14km (9 miles) wide. Accommodation ranges from luxurious colonial mansions to historic settlers' and miners' cottages, small motels and fully serviced caravan and tent sites.

The Barossa was founded by German Lutherans who arrived in 1842 fleeing religious persecution at home. The Germanic atmosphere became a real liability when Australia entered World War I. Some of the Teutonic place names were changed for 'patriotic' reasons, and the government shut down a German printing house for fear that it would produce subversive leaflets. Nowadays, the Germanic atmosphere pervading the valley is all part of the charm. You'll see neat stone cottages with filigreed verandahs and decorous gardens, and be able to taste *Bratwurst* and *Sauerkraut* to the accompaniment of oom-pah music.

The Barossa Valley is only about an hour's drive northeast of Adelaide, a perfect distance for an easy all-day excursion devoted to sniffing out the local colour and sampling the wines. Many of the wineries here offer guided tours (some departing from Adelaide) and tastings. Be warned that the vineyard route is so popular that the roads and cellars can get crowded on Sundays and public holidays. Every alternate year (the odd numbers) the Barossa Valley stages an ebullient Vintage Festival in March or April, a week-long carnival as earthy as the wines it celebrates.

The sun sets over the ranks of Barossa Valley vines

Kangaroo Island

South Australia's favourite escapist resort, **Kangaroo Island** is so big that you could spend a week finding the best places for swimming, fishing and sightseeing. Approximately 145km (90 miles) long and 30km (19 miles) wide, it's the country's third largest island, after Tasmania and the Northern Territory's Melville Island. For tourists in a typical rush, though, there are one-day excursions. It's only half an hour by air from Adelaide, but the most common route is by car ferry from Cape Jervis on the Flerieu Peninsula *(see page 156)* to the settlement of Penneshaw across the rough Backstairs Passage (a 45-minute trip each way).

The English explorer Matthew Flinders, who circumnavigated Australia at the beginning of the 19th century, chanced upon Kangaroo Island in a storm. His hungry crew, amazed to be met by a mob of fearless, friendly kangaroos, consigned some of the reception committee to the

Why 'Kangaroo'?

On one of his visits ashore, Captain James Cook asked an Aborigine what that strange leaping animal was. 'Kangaroo', came the reply. Cook passed on this intelligence to the whole world. An urban myth has it that the word *kangaroo* means 'I don't understand you' in an Aboriginal language; in fact, it comes from the word *gangurru*, meaning grey kangaroo.

There are around 45 species of kangaroos and wallabies, ranging in size from the red kangaroo, taller than a man, to the musky rat kangaroo, the size of a guinea-pig. Members of the family have adapted to many habitats: open plains, woodlands, rocky outcrops and cliffs – and some even climb trees. A young kangaroo, born in a near-embryonic state, crawls into its mother's pouch and attaches itself to a teat. It develops there for another four to eight months, depending on the species. Even when it is capable of venturing out it returns to the pouch between expeditions.

stew pot. Grateful for the sustenance, the great navigator named the place Kangaroo Island. Right behind the Flinders expedition came a French explorer called Nicolas Baudin. Despite having lost the territorial claim to the British, he mapped much of the island's coastline and contributed some French names to its features. They are still on the map: places such as D'Estrees Bay, Cape Du Couëdic and Cape D'Estaing. In later years, settlers

Australian sealions in Seal Bay

acknowledged Baudin's effort and built a white-domed monument to him at Hog Bay, called **Frenchman's Rock**.

The capital of Kangaroo Island, **Kingscote**, has a permanent population of around 1,800. Dolphins and seals can be seen frolicking just offshore, and there is a penguin colony nearby. The island is renowned for its unspoilt coastline of bays, cliffs and beaches. Its western end is taken up by **Flinders Chase National Park**, South Australia's biggest nature reserve. The animals there are in their natural state, but in the absence of predators the kangaroos, koalas and emus have become extroverts, trying to sponge or steal some food from the visitors. On the south coast, **Seal Bay** belongs to Australian sealions. They are so unafraid of humans that you can wander among them, guided by a national park ranger. Birdwatchers thrill to local species, which show clear differences from mainland relatives, and a noisy population of migratory birds from distant oceans.

Three Peninsulas

Just to the south of Adelaide, the **Fleurieu Peninsula** is an easy-to-reach, easy-to-like vacation land of surfing beaches, vineyards and history. The history starts at the beginning of the 19th century when the French explorer Baudin named the peninsula after his navy minister, Count Pierre de Fleurieu. The first industry to be based on the peninsula was whaling, centred on **Victor Harbor**. It's now the area's biggest town, and a very popular year-round resort.

Yet another historic location is **Maslins Beach** on the Gulf St Vincent coast. Here, in 1975, a new leaf was turned in the evolution of Australian social customs. This was the nation's first legal nudist beach. Now there are many to be found around the coastline.

Eyre Peninsula

Further inland, scores of vineyards basking in the sunshine of the Southern Vales are the reason for the peninsula's fame. They've been making wine here since 1838, to great effect. Many of the wineries encourage connoisseurs or simply wine drinkers to stop in and try the vintages. The best-known area of wine production is **McLaren Vale**.

The **Yorke Peninsula**, located west of Adelaide, first became important during the 19th century as a copper-mining district. The majority of the region's miners were drafted in from copper-rich Cornwall in England, and the Cornish touch can still be seen in the design of the old cottages and churches in the area. Museums and the ruins of the mine superstructures provide constant reminders of the peninsula's heyday, which continued until the 1920s. The locals have even kept up the tradition of baking Cornish pasties.

The **Eyre Peninsula** encompasses beach resorts, wheat fields, bushland, industrial centres and a prized wilderness, the **Lincoln National Park**. Set atop magnificent cliffs at the tip of the peninsula, the park is home to kangaroos and birds as diverse as emus, parrots and sea eagles. Fishing boats big and small are anchored in the attractive deepwater harbour of **Port Lincoln**, the tuna-fishing capital of Australia. Visit the home of the now-endangered great white shark on a cruise to Dangerous Reef.

Port Lincoln celebrates **Tunarama Festival** on the foreshore of Boston Bay each January over Australia Day weekend (26 January). Highlights include the World Record John West Tuna Tossing Championship, which sees world-class athletes turn up to throw large fish.

About an hour's drive west of Port Lincoln is **Coffin Bay National Park**, an unspoilt stretch of coast. Fishing and swimming are the main draws, and there are many isolated beaches and bays to explore.

The biggest city on the peninsula is **Whyalla**, which grew from a solid base of heavy industry – as heavy as iron and steel. If a blast furnace is your idea of fun, you can join one of the tours of the local steelworks (phone the visitor centre, tel: (08) 8645 7900); you can also visit the iron-mining area.

The Eyre Peninsula reaches as far west as **Ceduna**, where the vast expanse of the **Nullarbor Plain** begins. It's more than 1,200km (745 miles) from Ceduna westward to the next town of any significance (Norseman, WA). Filling stations do occur, but the route is lonely and gruelling. Nullarbor is sometimes thought of as an Aboriginal word. It's actually Latin for 'treeless', an indication that the plain is also waterless. But, as the Aboriginal inhabitants have always been aware, water is there if you know where to look for it: underground in limestone caverns. The highway follows the dunes and cliffs that lie along the length of the Great Australian Bight, which forms the bulk of the continent's curving southern coast.

The Flinders Ranges

For scenic splendour, South Australia's Outback competes well with the remote areas of the other states, nowhere more impressively than in the **Flinders Ranges**, 450km (280 miles) due north of Adelaide. Rising from a landscape as flat as the sea, the tinted peaks speak poetry to lovers of robust scenery. In the spring the rugged wooded hillsides come to life with a flood of wildflowers, but at any time of year the scene is intriguing. The mountains, like the desert, are much more colourful at close range.

An outstanding phenomenon found in the Flinders Ranges is a huge natural basin called **Wilpena Pound**. Rimmed by sheer cliffs, the saucer is approximately 20km (12 miles) long and 8km (5 miles) wide. Although it looks like a crater, it was actually formed by folding rocks. Wilpena Pound is not only spectacular as a scenic and a geological curiosity, it also wins admiring squawks from the birdwatchers. This is a place where you can spot species including butcherbirds, wagtails, galahs, honeyeaters and wedge-tailed eagles.

The flat floor of the Pound is perfectly designed for bush walks (suggested routes are signposted) – but not in summer, when it's altogether too hot for unnecessary exertion. In any season it's essential to carry a supply of drinking

Colourful vegetation at Wilpena Pound in the Flinders Ranges

water. There's only one way into the amphitheatre, through a narrow gorge occupied in rainy times by Wilpena Creek.

An area of such grandeur was bound to inspire Aboriginal myths and art over thousands of years. Timeless rock paintings can be inspected near Wilpena at Arkaroo, and at Yourambulla Cave, south of the village of **Hawker**.

Coober Pedy

The opal-mining town of **Coober Pedy** must rate as one of the most bizarre tourist attractions in the world. When you say 'desert' this is what it means: in the summer the daytime temperature can reach 50°C (122°F). That's in the shade, of which supplies are extremely limited. In the winter the nights become unpleasantly cold. Yet nearly 2,000 people make their home in this far corner of the Outback.

At first glance, the town looks very much like a hard-hit battlefield. The almost treeless terrain consists of hundreds

of mounds of upturned earth. But beneath the surface, things are not so bleak. The name Coober Pedy comes from an Aboriginal phrase meaning 'white fellow's hole in the ground' for the settlers have survived here by burrowing hobbit-like into the side of a low hill. The temperatures within are constant and comfortable, regardless of the excesses outside. Among the dugouts are residences of some luxury, with electricity and wall-to-wall carpets. Also underground are a Roman Catholic chapel,

What's an opal?

Opal is not a crystal but more like quartz, made up of silica with a small amount of water. Unlike diamonds, opals are used only for jewellery.

several motels and B&Bs, a café, a restaurant, a bookshop, opal shops, museums and a pottery shop.

Regular tours by bus or plane bring the curious crowds to Coober Pedy, which is about 950km (590 miles) northwest of Adelaide. The tours visit underground homes as well as the local opal fields, where most of the world's opals are mined, with demonstrations of opal cutting and polishing. Having learned the intricacies, you can buy finished stones and jewellery on the spot. Or try noodling in the mullock heaps: all you need is a rake or a sieve to sift through the rubble at the top of each mineshaft, and if you're lucky you may find an overlooked opal. No permit is required for non-profit fossicking, although you must obtain the permission of the landholder first. Tours to Coober Pedy also explore the desolate desert landscape outside town.

VICTORIA

By Australian standards, the state of Victoria is a midget. About the same size as Great Britain, it is the smallest state on the mainland. But its more than 5 million inhabitants give Victoria Australia's highest population density.

Over 70 percent of Victorians live in the capital, Melbourne, a centre for finance, industry, culture and sport. The city folk live within easy striking distance of the state's bushland and 19th-century boomtowns, the sea, the vineyards and the ski slopes. Some of the scenery is so rich and pretty that the state's first name was Australia Felix – Latin for bountiful or lucky. For tourists, the state's relatively small size and varied landscapes make for convenient exploration.

Victoria was the earliest state to industrialise, but it's still a leading farming power as well – hence the nickname of

Melbourne, looking along the Yarra River towards the CBD

'Garden State'. This agricultural potential remained unexploited until the 1860s, after the state's gold rush fizzled out. Unemployed ex-prospectors eagerly fanned out as farmers, working land they bought for £1 per acre. Immigrants in search of a figurative pot of gold followed in a steady flow that reached a tidal wave after World War II, with the policy of 'populate or perish'. This produced both curious ethnic pockets around the state and the cosmopolitan effervescence of a multicultural society within the dignified confines of the capital city.

Melbourne

Elegant parks and gardens splash green patterns across the map of **Melbourne**, softening the rigours of its precise grid plan, and offering merciful breathing space on the edges of the city centre's hubbub. This is a friendly city of serious buildings and imposing Victorian architecture. Its air of distinction may have something to do with the fact that the city was founded

It Could Have Been Batmania

Australia's second city could have had a rather foolish or embarrassing name if the Governor of New South Wales, Sir Richard Bourke, had not been a traditionalist. The first settlement of tents and huts on the Yarra had been called Bearbrass, for reasons that are not entirely clear. Yarra Yarra was also suggested as a possible name for the growing town, and so was Batmania, in honour of J. Batman, a settler from Tasmania who bought 40,000 hectares (100,000 acres) from the Aborigines. (The fact that he bought the territory, albeit at a derisory price, rather than simply stealing it, was a rare occurrence for the period.) But when Bourke visited the region in 1837, he decreed that the town should be named, in the customary fashion, after a British dignitary – in this case the Prime Minister, Lord Melbourne.

not by prisoners (as was Sydney) but by adventurous free enterprisers with their own vision of success.

It's all so grand you might forget Melbourne's rough-and-tumble pioneering days. The gold rush broke out in Victoria in 1851, only a few months after the fever hit New South Wales. A gold strike at Ballarat so electrified the state that Melbourne itself risked becoming a ghost town; businessmen locked their offices or shops

Melburnians love sports

and rushed to the goldfields, and ships were abandoned by their gold-crazed crews. New immigrants rushing in to fill the gap lived in shacks and tents. Successful diggers, on their return to Melbourne, had so much money to dispose of that morals loosened considerably.

Australia's two largest cities, Sydney and Melbourne, have always been fierce rivals. Fans of Sydney think Melbourne is boring; those of Melbourne think Sydney is brash and superficial. Sydneysiders blast Melbourne's climate; Melburnians ridicule Sydney's self-satisfaction. Generally, Melbourne (population about 3.8 million) seems to be on the defensive, for instance about the unpredictable weather, but can point to several international surveys that rank the city highly in terms of quality of life.

If Melbourne is staid, as Sydneysiders allege, you'd never know it from their sports mania. 'Footy' – or Australian Rules Football – is the main attraction here. Cricket is also a passion. And as for the horses, the Melbourne Cup is so all-engrossing that the first Tuesday in November, when the race is run, counts as a legal holiday. The 2006 Commonwealth Games were held in Melbourne, whose residents packed the games' events.

In the last couple of decades of the 20th century, Melbourne was a city that emptied after dark, but all that has changed dramatically. Residents have moved back into the inner city, and the Central Business District now has cafés, bars and nightclubs. Melburnians have something of a reputation as gourmets and, with some 3,000 restaurants in the city, they are spoilt for choice.

Crossing the Yarra towards Eureka Skydeck 88

City Sights

A pleasant aspect of Melbourne can be viewed from the level of the **Yarra**, the river at the centre of the city. On the last few kilometres of its journey to the sea, the Yarra plays host to freighters, pleasure boats and rowing regattas. And it waters the gardens, reflects the skyscrapers and invites cyclists and joggers to follow its course along pretty paths. For a look up at the skyline and a close-up of river commerce, take one of the cruise boats that leave from **Princes Walk** by **Princes Bridge**.

Aerial views over the river and the city point up the ample hectares of green in the parks and gardens in among the business-like blocks. The best vantage point is the observation deck of **Eureka Skydeck 88** (open daily 10am–9.30om; admission fee), 285m (935ft) above **Southbank**, a riverside shopping and strolling precinct on the southern bank of the Yarra. The view extends beyond West-gate Bridge to the west, the Dandenong Ranges to the east and the shimmering expanse of Port Phillip Bay to the south. Those with a good head for heights can try Skydeck's **The Edge** (additional fee), a huge glass cube jutting out of the building, which gives those inside a feeling of hanging in mid-air.

Also at Southbank is the enormous **Crown Entertainment Complex**, housing the 500-room Crown Towers Hotel and Crown Casino. The casino is one of the country's largest gaming establishments.

Just past the Crown complex and the soon-to-open Melbourne Exhibition and Convention Centre is the *Polly Woodside*, a square-rigged sailing barque, recalling the adventurous days of the last century. Launched in Ireland in 1885, the restored ship is now part of a maritime museum (closed for renovations).

If you walk a little way downriver and cross over a footbridge, you'll find yourself in **Melbourne Docklands** (you can also get here on a free City Circle tram from central Melbourne). An ambitious urban renewal programme is taking place at this former port, which has Victoria Harbour at its heart. Already there are parklands, marinas, apartments, offices, shops, bars, cafés, restaurants and leisure facilities, including the huge Telstra Dome. One attraction still taking shape is a giant observation wheel, similar to the London Eye.

Near the river, just south of the heart of town, on St Kilda Road, an Eiffel Tower-style superstructure marks the modern **Victorian Arts Centre**. This airy silver, gold and white spire rises from flowing curves suggesting a ballet dancer's tutu. The first part of the complex to open, in 1968, was the

National Gallery of Victoria, which has been renamed **NGV International** (open Wed–Mon 10am–5pm; <www.ngv.vic.gov.au>; free). The large collection showcases international (that is, non-Australian) art, old and new. Among the most choice items on display are a vast Tiepolo painting from the 1740s, *The Banquet of Cleopatra*; sculptures by Rodin, Henry Moore and Barbara Hepworth; and a first-class survey of classical Chinese porcelain. The Ian Potter Centre, at Federation Square, houses the Gallery's wealth of Australian art *(see page 167)*.

The **Theatres Building**, directly beneath the symbolic spire identifying the Arts Centre, is the place for opera, ballet and musicals. Under the same roof are a playhouse for drama and a smaller studio theatre for performances of more intimate works. The adjoining, circular **Hamer Hall**, which seats 2,700 people, is used for symphony concerts, but the acoustics can be changed to suit other types of performance. If you're not going to a concert, nip in for a glance at the artwork in the lobby, or take a guided backstage tour. The complex provides dining opportunities from snack bars to luxury-class restaurants. The Centre also includes a Museum of Performing Arts.

Just across Princes Bridge on the north side of the river, the spires of **St Paul's Cathedral** are not as old as they look. They were added in the 1920s, several decades after the original Gothic-style structure was completed. The church is a refreshing hideaway in the midst of the busiest part of the business district, a few steps away from the Victorian mass of the main suburban railway station, Flinders Street Station, and a less obvious historic landmark, **Young and Jackson's** pub. In the bar upstairs hangs a notorious oil painting of the nude 'Chloe', which has delighted many generations of beer drinkers since it scandalised Melbourne's art exhibition of 1880. By today's standards, it's quite staid.

Just north of St Paul's Cathedral is **Federation Square**, a futuristic-looking group of modern buildings built around a public square. Along with various recreational amenities, it houses the **Ian Potter Centre: NGV Australia** (open Tues–Sun 10am–5pm; <www.ngv.vic.gov.au>; free), a stunning three-floor space with 20 galleries dedicated to Australian art – contemporary, colonial and indigenous.

The **Town Hall**, on the opposite side of Collins Street, dates from the 1860s. It is used for concerts and official events, and can hold some 3,000 people.

In Federation Square

Collins Street, the parallel Bourke Street and Bourke Street's arcades and laneways are the reason Melburnians claim to have the best shopping in Australia. Two large department stores – Myer and David Jones – are located close together in pedestrians-only **Bourke Street Mall**. The outstanding example of an old-time Melbourne shopping institution, the glass-roofed **Block Arcade** is an 1892 copy of Milan's Vittorio Emmanuele Galleria. Have afternoon tea at the historic Hopetoun Tea Rooms inside the arcade. The nearby Royal Arcade is also worth investigating. Also running off Bourke Street Mall are narrow laneways lined with avant garde boutiques and numerous cafés, part of the city's well-developed coffee culture. Try Cathedral Arcade or

Flinders Way for the best of independent and local fashion designers. One end of the mall is dominated by the Victorian-era Melbourne GPO, which has been renovated as a hub for sophisticated fashion and food shopping.

By way of historic buildings, Melbourne likes to show off **Parliament House**, set in its own park facing Spring Street. It has been called the finest legislative headquarters this side of London; in fact, many of the furnishings found here are copies of those in Britain's Palace of Westminster. The federal government used this as its temporary headquarters in the early 20th century, just after Federation. The building is open for guided tours when the state parliament is not sitting.

Older than any of the city's well-preserved Victorian buildings is **Captain Cook's Cottage** in Fitzroy Gardens. The great discoverer never lived in Melbourne; the stone house was transplanted in 1934 from Great Ayton in Cook's native

One of central Melbourne's many laneways

Yorkshire. In truth, it would be more accurate to call it Cook's parents' cottage, since there is no evidence that the good captain ever lived in it.

Only in Australia, it seems, are jails such popular tourist attractions. The most fascinating of all is the **Old Melbourne Gaol** (open daily 9.30am–5pm; <www.oldmelbournegaol. com.au>; admission fee), situated just across the street from the modern Police Headquarters on Russell Street. Opened in 1854, the penitentiary was the scene of more than 100 hangings. The death masks of the most famous prisoners are displayed, along with other penal memorabilia, such as a 'lashing triangle', last used in 1958. The best-known character on death row, the celebrated bushranger Ned Kelly, was executed here on Melbourne Cup Day 1880. The jail displays the weird suit of improvised armor he was wearing when captured. And you can step inside the executive-sized cell that was his last residence on earth; it has a fine view of the gallows.

Within walking distance north of the city centre is the **Royal Exhibition Building**, a beautiful leftover from the 1880 Melbourne International Exhibition. Next to it is a much more modern building housing the **Melbourne Museum** (open daily 10am–4.30pm; <www.museumvictoria. com.au>; admission fee), which is devoted to history, natural history and ethnography. Exhibits include an impressive indoor rainforest, dinosaur skeletons, an Aboriginal culture gallery and a gallery of boats of the Pacific islands.

Melbourne's **Chinatown** centres on Little Bourke Street, to the east of Swanston Street. Special street lights and gates define the area, in which you'll find Chinese restaurants jammed shoulder to shoulder with cafés, a church, small factories and exotic shops. The area has had a unique flavour since the gold rush days, when fortune-hunters from China crowded into this low-rent district before and after their efforts out in the bush. Chinatown today glows on the maps of local gourmets.

So does **Queen Victoria Market**, which sums up the bounty of Australian agriculture. Just about everything that grows can be found here, piled up in irresistibly fresh pyramids. It's as if the best fruit and vegetables had been borrowed from every market from Sweden to Sicily. The best time to take in the atmosphere is early in the morning, but note that Queen Victoria Market is closed on Mondays and Wednesdays. In addition to produce, you will find a flea market.

Parks and Gardens

South of the river are the **Royal Botanic Gardens** (open 7.30am–dusk), classed among the finest in the world. Thirty-six hectares (90 acres) of superb rolling landscape remind the visitor that Melbourne has four seasons. Each time of year has its specialities, and seasonal leaflets are available for self-guide walks. For Australians, some of the joy of this park is the selection of brightly tinted trees and plants collected from the Northern Hemisphere. A total of 13,000 species are represented here, in addition to the lovely lawns and lakes.

Between the Botanic Gardens and Kings Domain is **Government House**, the state governor's mansion, and **La Trobe's Cottage**, its early 19th-century predecessor. The timber cottage was shipped over from Britain to serve as a home for Charles La Trobe, who became Victoria's first Lieutenant-Governor back in 1851. One of La Trobe's achievements was to establish a wine industry in Victoria.

Across from the cottage, the massive **Shrine of Remembrance** (open daily 10am–5pm) was originally built in remembrance of the dead of World War I, but now commemorates those Australians who have fallen in armed conflicts in general. Once a year, every Armistice Day at 11am, a beam of sunlight coming through an opening in the roof strikes the Rock of Remembrance. It is a powerful and poignant experience.

In Parkville, located to the north of the centre, the **Royal Melbourne Zoological Gardens** (open daily 9am–5pm; admission fee) have kangaroos, koalas and platypuses, plus elephants, giraffes, monkeys and other creatures from far-flung countries. In summer, there's musical entertainment.

Melbourne's Suburbs

The inner-city suburb of **Carlton** – a short tram trip from the city – combines the restored elegance of Victorian architecture with contemporary dynamism. The latter may be attributed to the area's immigrant colony, mostly Italian. Hence there

Autumn comes to the Royal Botanic Gardens

is a great profusion of outdoor cafés, pizzerias, trattorias, pasticcerias and gelaterias.

Lygon Street, Carlton, is Melbourne's very own slice of Italy, replete with numerous pasta restaurants interspersed with wine bars, cheese shops, quality fashion boutiques and delicatessens. Jimmy Watson's bar and restaurant in Lygon Street is a Melbourne institution.

In **South Yarra**, about 2 hectares (5 acres) of lawns and gardens surround Melbourne's finest stately home, **Como House** (open daily 10am–5pm; admission fee). Now run by the National Trust, this example of the colonial era's high style was completed with the addition of a gold-and-white ballroom in the 1870s. Each of its two stories was built with wide verandahs decorated with intricate ironwork.

Toorak, the snootiest of suburbs, is rumoured to harbour more money than any other suburb in Australia. The mansions make tourists and most other passers-by stand and gape. Shopping on Toorak Road is full of stylish delights.

A totally different shopping experience awaits in the seaside suburb of **St Kilda**. On Sundays its Esplanade is taken over by artists, antiques dealers and flea market entrepreneurs of every sort. Acland Street's restaurants, cafés and bakeries preserve a middle-European Jewish flavour.

Brunswick Street, in **Fitzroy**, reflects the city's bohemian side. Restaurants and cafés, Spanish bars on nearby Johnston Street, comedy and live-band venues – all buzzing with activity day and night. Fitzroy's streets are crammed with alternative lifestyle shops, second-hand clothing and funky furniture.

Excursions

A favourite day trip from Melbourne goes out to the **Dandenong Ranges**, volcanic mountains where flowered hillsides and eucalyptus forests set the scene for total relaxation. Only an hour's drive from town, the mountains won't exactly take your breath away; Mt Dandenong itself claims an altitude of only 633m (2,077ft).

One highlight of a day among the small towns, farms, parks and gardens of the Dandenongs is a ride on **Puffing Billy**, a restored old steam train plying 13km (8 miles) of narrow-gauge track from Belgrave to Menzies Creek. The line was given over to passenger operations from 1900 to 1958. Four years later it was converted to the tourism business. The train never achieves great speed. In fact, an annual race pits Puffing Billy against hundreds of runners.

The **William Ricketts Sanctuary** (open daily 10am–4.30pm; admission fee) is an extraordinary collection of sculpture produced by a caucasian loner who became obsessed with Aboriginal culture and its near-destruction by his fellow whites. Ricketts carved incredibly lifelike faces of Aboriginal people, accompanied by their spiritual symbols. The result of his artistic toils is unorthodox, even unnerving.

In **Sherbrooke Forest Park**, part of Dandenong Ranges National Park, you can give your lungs a treat, savouring the elixir of ferns and mountain ash and whatever flowers happen to be in bloom. The forest is immensely tall, with mountain ash monuments as high

Puffing Billy's conductor

as 20-storey buildings and ferns as big as palm trees. This is the place to see – or at least hear – the lyrebird, a great mimic; it does imitations of other birds, human voices and even of inanimate objects such as passing cars. Among the animal residents of the park are the echidna, alias the spiny anteater, the platypus and the koala.

Healesville, less than 60km (37 miles) to the east of Melbourne, is the place to go for an intimate look at Australian animals on their home ground. **Healesville Sanctuary**, nearby in the **Yarra Valley** (open daily 9am–5pm; admission fee), contains more than 200 native species such as kangaroos, wombats and emus. The sanctuary was founded in 1921 as a research establishment for the study of local fauna, and is committed to the care of Australian wildlife and the conservation of endangered species.

The Yarra Valley was the site of the first commercial winery in the state, dating back to the middle of the 19th century. The region's vineyards, numbering about 80, are world-class; well worth a wine-tasting outing or a visit to one of the winery restaurants.

Another wine region near Melbourne is the **Mornington Peninsula**, an 80-minute drive south of the city. In addition to the 50 wineries with cellar doors, there are beaches, national parks, coastal walking trails, lovely rural scenery and pleasant villages such as Red Hill, Shoreham and Flinders.

Phillip Island lookout

Phillip Island

For a magical experience for both adults and children, try a long day-trip to **Phillip Island**, 120km (75 miles) southeast of Melbourne, home of the fairy penguins (also known as little penguins), the world's smallest members of the penguin family. Hundreds of these engaging birds, standing only about 40cm (16in) high and looking quite formal in their blue-grey plumage with white fronts, come home to their burrows at sunset. The number varies depending on activities at sea, where they spend most of their time fishing.

For reasons of their own, perhaps sensing danger, they tread water offshore until night falls, and only then do they venture onto the beach. After decades of being stared at by visitors, they still feel insecure arriving on the island.

Little penguin

Before dusk falls, hundreds of tourists gather behind ropes on Summerland Beach and in viewing platforms on the sandhills above. You're not allowed to do anything that might upset the penguins: no flash photography, no running, no sudden movement. The penguins observe all this and wait for the first star to appear in the sky.

Then the first brave penguin scout scrambles onto dry land and suspiciously lurches across the beach and up the hill to his burrow. In small groups the others follow, waddling through the sand dunes up to their burrows right at sunset, just as their ancestors have done night after night for thousands of generations. It can take half an hour or more for all the birds that are coming ashore to arrive.

The penguins are the stars, but the supporting cast is also well worth seeing: thousands of fur seals residing on tall rocks on the west coast (early December, the peak of the breeding season, is the best time to see them); clouds of mutton birds arriving each November from their wintering grounds thousands of kilometres away; and a colony of koalas, vegetating in the high branches of the gum trees. Take a sweater or coat for the penguin parade, for the nights are chilly even in summer.

Wilsons Promontory

Until the Ice Age, the southernmost tip of the Australian mainland was connected to Tasmania. When the ice melted the heights became an island. Since then the dunes have built up, linking the massive promontory to the rest of Victoria. The varied and spectacular scenery has made **Wilsons Promontory** the state's most popular national park.

The coastline ranges from magnificent granite headlands to peaceful sandy beaches. Walking trails wander through forests and moorland and flower-covered heathland. Koalas live here, as do kangaroos and emus. Known locally as 'The Prom', the peninsula is about 240km (150 miles) southeast of Melbourne.

The Goldfields

A drive of 113km (70 miles) west of Melbourne takes you well over a century back in time to the town of **Ballarat**, rich with all the atmosphere of Australia's golden age. This is real gold-rush country, and it is still a prize destination for tourists.

Ballarat has a bittersweet history. Gold was discovered in 1851, and thousands of miners trekked to the fields. The early arrivals simply scooped up a fortune, but latecomers had to work harder, following the ore ever deeper.

Almost from the outset the government collected a licence fee from the miners. Many newcomers couldn't afford to pay a tax, so they tended to lie low when the licence inspectors swooped. In the midst of growing antagonism between the authorities and the miners, charges of murder and official corruption pushed the diggers to revolt. In the Eureka Rebellion, Australia's first and only uprising, insurgent miners were besieged in their stockade. An uneven battle cost 35 people their lives, mostly diggers. The nation was stunned. The anguish endured for years, inspiring poets and politicians.

When peace returned to the goldfields, and many of the miners' grievances were answered, Ballarat went back to the business of making a fortune. In 1858 a group of Cornishmen came upon what they called the Welcome Nugget, weighing in at an enormous 63,000g (2,220oz). It was eventually put on show in the Crystal Palace in London before being minted. Parallel with the discovery of wealth, Ballarat grew into a stately town where even art and good taste had their day.

To see what Ballarat was like in the 1850s, visit **Sovereign Hill** (open daily 10am–5pm; <www.sovereignhill.com.au>; admission fee), an open-air museum recreating the sights, sounds and smells of the gold rush. Local people dressed in Victorian-era clothing operate the old shops, post office, bakery and printing office of what appears to be a real town. Tourists are invited to try their hand with a digger's pan. The **Gold Museum** (open daily 9.30am–5.20pm; admission fee) traces the history of the mineral since biblical times and displays nuggets and gold coins.

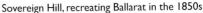

Sovereign Hill, recreating Ballarat in the 1850s

In the real Ballarat, the principal public buildings on the town's wide tree-lined streets are a long-lasting monument to the good old days. Some of those who got rich quick had the good taste to spend some of their money on the finer things. Hence the statues of mythological subjects in marble in the **Botanical Gardens**, and the admirable collection of early Australian art housed in the **Ballarat Fine Arts Gallery** (open daily 10.30am–5pm; admission fee).

Another treat for nostalgia fans is the town of **Bendigo**, situated 150km (93 miles) northwest of Melbourne. The town's unusual name is a very roundabout corruption of Abednego, the Old Testament companion of Shadrach and Meshach. In the 1850s, Bendigo Creek, running through the centre of town, was besieged with panning miners.

Life was tough in the mines

The **Central Deborah Mine** (open daily 9.30am–5pm; admission fee), the last commercial mine to operate in Bendigo, is now a museum of 19th-century mining technology; a visit includes a one-hour underground mine tour. From the mine you can take a 'Talking Tram', an antique vehicle rigged up for tourists on an 8-km (5-mile) historic itinerary. The last stop is the **joss house**. One curiosity of Bendigo was the size of the Chinese population. Chinese miners, who enjoyed less than harmony with their white neighbours, worshipped in a prayer house constructed of timber and handmade bricks. The remains that stand today are filled with relics of the early Chinese fortune hunters.

The Great Ocean Road

Beyond **Torquay** is the beginning of the **Great Ocean Road**, which skirts nearly 200km (125 miles) of spectacular coastline and is undoubtedly one of the world's most beautiful drives. It was built by ex-serviceman of the World War I in homage to their comrades killed at the front.

A great number of ships have gone aground in these treacherous waters. Along **Shipwreck Coast**, the wrecks of more than 80 sailing vessels rest on the seabed. Rising above the road are the bush-covered Otway Ranges, most of which fall within **Great Otway National Park**, which has many bushwalking options. The surf provides recreation, too: **Bells Beach**, situated between Torquay and Anglesea, hosts the Bells Surfing Classic every Easter. Just before you reach Lorne, follow the signs for **Erskine Falls**, splendid cascades which are worth the 20-minute detour. **Lorne** and, further west, **Apollo Bay** are popular seaside resorts, well provided with restaurants, cafés and shops. From Apollo Bay, the Great Ocean Road leaves the coast to wind through the forest behind **Cape Otway**, where the lighthouse has watched over the entrance to the Bass Strait since 1848.

Beyond Princetown lies the spectacular coastline of **Port Campbell National Park**, where breakers have battered the soft limestone cliffs, creating grottoes and gorges, arches and sea-sculptures rising from the surf. The Great Ocean Road allows only occasional glimpses of the drama below, which includes the stark rock stacks known as the **Twelve Apostles** and the spray billowing through **London Arch**. Take the time to stop at all the vantage points.

After Peterborough and the spectacular Bay of Islands comes **Warrnambool**, once a busy port and now a pastoral and holiday centre. Around the original lighthouse is the **Flagstaff Hill Maritime Museum** (open daily 9am–5pm; admission fee), a recreation of a 19th-century port with its shipwrights, chandlers and sailmakers.

Along the coast is the fishing-village charm of **Port Fairy**, where brightly painted boats tie up at the jetty with their catches of lobster and crab. Traditionally the birthplace of Victoria, Port Fairy was named by Captain James Wishart who brought his tiny cutter, the *Fairy*, into the Moyne River to find shelter during a sealing expedition in 1810. Sealers and, later, whalers built quaint stone cottages which still nestle under the tall Norfolk Island pines shading the streets. In March each year, a very popular three-day folk festival draws music lovers to the town.

Along the Great Ocean Road

TASMANIA

If you thought of Tasmania as the last stop before the South Pole, you're right: Antarctic expeditions actually set sail from Hobart. No matter what direction you're heading in, it's a staging post you will hate to leave. Tasmania's scenery owes more to solar than polar influences. Although

Rustic charm in Tasmania

snow covers the hills in winter, it's a verdant island enjoying a temperate climate.

Suspended 240km (149 miles) to the south of southernmost mainland Australia, Tasmania is small only by the swollen standards of the continent. With an area of approximately 68,000 sq km (26,250 sq miles), it's bigger than Sri Lanka or Switzerland.

'Tassie', as the state is familiarly known, calls itself the Holiday Isle and pushes tourism. Its early residents would have had a bitter laugh at that, interspersed with an oath or two, for the island used to be the place where the really incorrigible prisoners were sent. While humble embezzlers and petty larcenists were transported to Sydney, the batterers and escape artists tended to be tagged for Tasmania.

Early explorers happened upon Tasmania because it lies on the 40th parallel – the Roaring Forties – along which an unfailing westerly wind blows around the globe. Their sailing ships could hardly miss the place. But that's not to diminish the achievement of the Dutch navigator Abel Tasman, who discovered the island in 1642. He named it after his sponsor, Anton van Diemen, governor of the Dutch East Indies.

The Dutch never saw a future for Van Diemen's Land, and Britain eventually claimed the island simply to cut out the French. Because of the cruel conditions inflicted on the British prisoners, Van Diemen's Land acquired a sinister reputation. The very mention of the name could send a shiver down a sinner's spine. The transportation of convicts was abolished in 1852, and some three years later the name was changed to Tasmania in memory of its discoverer and to improve the state's image.

Since then, Tasmania has become something of a tourist paradise. One day, some brilliant entrepreneur may put it on the world map and the crowds will arrive. Until then, however, if you like wild scenery, open moors, rolling green hills, deserted beaches, Georgian architecture, temperate-climate forests, uncrowded towns and open-hearted people, you could easily become a Tasmaniac.

Wiping out the Aborigines

When Van Diemen's Land was first settled, the island's Aboriginal people are estimated to have numbered between 3,000 and 7,000. They were different from the indigenous mainland peoples, in looks and culture. As the British seized the land and wiped out the animals and birds that the indigenous tribes needed for food, the Aborigines fought back with punitive attacks. Enraged, the white men retaliated with all the force at their disposal. The survivors of this pogrom were exiled to Flinders Island, in the Bass Strait, an outpost best known for its shipwrecks. Although there were belated efforts to protect the race, the last of the full-blooded Tasmanian tribespeople died in 1876. The race was not entirely exterminated, however, as mixed-blood descendants of the Aboriginal women who had been abducted by British and American whalers and sealers and taken to islands in the Bass Strait (including Flinders) founded a flourishing Aboriginal movement.

Hobart

Everybody knows that Sydney Harbour is the exciting one, glamorous and instantly recognisable the world over. Hobart is the lovable harbour, a perfect ocean port on the Derwent River, with soft mountains rising beyond. It might have been transplanted from quite another seafaring latitude, as brisk and tidy as Bergen or Helsinki.

Hobart's General Post Office

You never know what kind of ships you'll see here: freighters from Singapore, floating fish factories from Japan, or yachts from distant islands – perhaps Britain or Bermuda. The arrival of an ancient sealer, whaler or windjammer in the harbour would be right in character. Sail power still matters here: Hobart's Constitution Dock is the finishing line of the gruelling Sydney to Hobart yacht race.

Hobart, Australia's second oldest capital city, has kept a powerful array of historic monuments, from stately official buildings to quaint cottages. Best of all, they're spick and span and still in use.

With a population of around 205,000 (suburbs included), Hobart is small enough to get around and get to know, and as unsophisticated and satisfying as the local fish and chips.

In this deepwater port, the ships come right into the centre of town, to **Sullivans Cove**. The waterfront, always colourful, is the place to begin exploring the city on foot or by taking a cruise from Brooke Street. You can watch crates of giant crabs, lobsters and scallops coming ashore, and

Boats moored in Hobart Harbour

follow their destiny to the floating fast-food restaurants moored at **Constitution Dock**, where the yacht races end. There's a big choice of waterfront bars, cafés and restaurants, mostly fish-themed, alongside and at trendy Elizabeth Street pier and lively Murray Street pier.

Also bordering the docks, **Salamanca Place** is home to a long row of sandstone warehouses from the 1830s, now occupied by artisans' workshops, boutiques and restaurants. On Saturday, the huge **Salamanca Market** (8.30am–3pm) takes over, with stalls selling various arts and crafts, knick-knacks, flowers and vegetables; buskers perform and pass the hat. Behind Salamanca Place, Salamanca Square is fringed with lively al fresco cafés, restaurants and bars.

Altogether more serious is **Parliament House**, built in 1840, also facing the waterfront. The state's bicameral legislature operates in a low-rise stone building which displays some admirable architectural details.

Another venerable structure still in use is the **Theatre Royal** on Campbell Street, Australia's oldest live theatre. Built in the most exquisitely luxurious style in 1834, it has featured stars like Noel Coward and Laurence Olivier.

Overlooking Salamanca Place, and reached on foot by Kelly's Steps, **Battery Point** is the historic heart of Hobart, beautifully preserved. The battery in question was a set of coastal artillery guns installed in 1818. Ten years later signal flags were added, for relaying the big news of the day, such as ship arrivals or prison escapes. The area is worth an hour or two of exploration on foot, to absorb the atmosphere of the narrow streets, the mansions and cottages, churches and taverns. National Trust volunteers lead excellent walking tours (bookings, tel: (03) 6344 6233).

One of the colonial mansions is now the **Narryna Heritage Museum** (open Tues–Fri 10.30am–5pm, Sat–Sun 2–5pm; admission fee), with period furnishings, vintage vehicles and various farm implements.

The **Tasmanian Museum and Art Gallery** (open daily 10am–5pm; <www.tmag.tas.gov.au>; free) is worth visiting for the collection relating to the Tasmanian tiger (thylacine). This striped, dog-like marsupial is believed to have been hunted to extinction by the 1930s, but some people swear they have seen living ones. If you prefer marine exhibits, visit the **Maritime Museum of Tasmania** (open daily 9am–5pm; <www.maritimetas.org>; admission fee), in Argyle Street.

The centre of Hobart is linked to the suburbs and the airport by the graceful **Tasman Bridge** across the Derwent River. The pre-stressed concrete bridge ran into trouble in 1975; more accurately, trouble ran into the bridge. A bulk ore carrier, off course, ploughed into the span of the bridge; tragically, four cars tumbled into the river and the ship sank.

For an expansive panorama of Hobart and the valley of the Derwent River, ascend **Mt Wellington**, the city's most prominent landmark. It is named in appreciation of the Duke of Wellington. For this expedition you can forget your mountain-climbing equipment. A paved road goes all the way to the summit, 1,270m (4,167ft) above the sea. It often snows on the mountain in the winter months – an exciting novelty for tourists from more northerly Australian climes – but it rarely blocks the road.

Excursions from Hobart

A popular tourist destination up the river at Claremont is the **Cadbury chocolate factory** (guided tours Mon–Fri). Fans of Willy Wonka just love it – and guided tours include as much chocolate as you can eat. The tours attract sweet-toothed visitors of all ages.

Those with a more savoury tooth might prefer touring the imposing **Cascade Brewery** (daily guided tours), the oldest in Australia, at 140 Cascade Road. The beer, made with pure Tasmanian water, is excellent. Cascade uses a Tasmanian tiger logo in its advertising and on its labels.

At **Taroona**, situated beyond Wrest Point Casino at up-market Sandy Bay, you can visit the remains, well over a century old, of a different kind of factory, the **Shot Tower**. Though it looks like an ordinary chimney, this 48-m (157-ft) high tower, built in 1870, was used in the manufacture of gunshot and musket balls. You can climb the internal spiral staircase (300 or so steps) to the very summit for a view of the countryside and the Derwent Estuary.

A complex of modern office buildings at **Kingston** is the working headquarters for Australia's extensive operations in the neighbourhood of the South Pole. The Commonwealth Antarctic Division coordinates logistics and research in fields such as glaciology, botany, physics and medicine. Inside the main building are displays of sleds and faded flags from the early pioneering expeditions.

Victorian buildings in Launceston

Launceston

Tasmania's second city is an agreeable, roomy town at the head of the Tamar River. Launceston exudes an unexpected English flavour, with elm trees, rosebushes, and patriotic statues and plaques. The journey north from Hobart skirts soft green hills studded with sheep. In the villages, to enliven the scene, the houses have roofs the colour of fire engines.

Launceston was founded in the year 1805 as Patersonia. Soon afterwards, the name was changed to that of the town of Launceston in Cornwall, the birthplace of the colony's governor. The historic aspects of the town are well preserved, starting in the centre, the **Civic Square**, the location of the **Macquarie House** (1830). Restored to mint condition, this sometime warehouse, barracks and office building is now a café.

The main building of the **Queen Victoria Museum** (open daily 10am–5pm; free), situated just a short stroll away on Wellington Street, has something for everyone, from stuffed platypuses to blunderbusses and prisoners' chains. One surprising attraction here is an intact joss house which originally served the Chinese tin miners in the Tasmanian town of Weldborough. Downstairs, the Queen Vic Café is one of Launceston's best. The museum's art collection has moved to the striking new Inveresk site, a multi-million-dollar transformation of a railway yard on the North Esk River.

Tasmania is known for its talented craftspeople, whose output is on show at the **Design Centre** (open Mon–Sat 9.30am–5.30pm, Sun 10.30am–3.30pm; admission fee), on the western edge of City Park. The highlight is the collection of contemporary furniture and other wood pieces made from various species of Tasmanian timber.

The **Cataract Gorge**, a stirring geological feature, is within walking distance of the centre of town. Here the South Esk River slices between steep cliffs on its way to the Tamar. There are hiking trails, boating opportunities and, for sightseers who don't suffer queasy spells, a chairlift – the longest single-span lift in the world at 308m (336yds) – spans the canyon from on high. Nearby is the **Boag's Centre for Beer Lovers** (open Mon–Fri 8.45am–4.30pm; free), housed in the historic Tamar Hotel, where you can take a tour of the brewery that makes one of Tasmania's – and Australia's – best beers (for tour bookings, tel: (03) 6332 6300).

Port Arthur

Tasmania's most-visited historic highlight is the old penal colony of **Port Arthur** (open daily 8.30am–dusk; <www.portarthur.org.au>; admission fee), an hour's drive from

Hobart on the scenic Tasman Peninsula. Port Arthur's past is so grim, you'll be astonished at just how picturesque it looks. Founded in 1830 as Australia's ultimate prison settlement, Port Arthur housed the most troublesome and intractable convicts – those who had committed second offences after being transported to Australia. It rapidly became one of the world's most-dreaded institutions, reputedly even more brutal than the French penal colony of Devil's Island in South America.

Chain gangs, toiling under the lash, built the stone buildings you see here, which have survived more than a century of neglect, fire, storm and looting. The fascinating story is detailed at the visitor centre, as well as in the compelling **museum** in what used to be the penal colony's asylum.

Port Arthur

The biggest building still standing, at four storeys high, was designed originally as a storehouse but became a penitentiary for 650 inmates. Other surviving buildings are the **Asylum** (many prisoners went mad) and, next door, the '**Model Prison**'. Both have been restored. Convicts designed and built a large church, now in picturesque ruins. Its 13 spires represent Christ and the apostles. Then there is the mortuary, which did a lively business; more than 1,700 graves occupy the nearby **Isle of the Dead**.

Other than by dying, Port Arthur was practically escape-proof, with sharks waiting on one side of the narrow Eagle-hawk Neck and half-starved killer dogs on the other. In total, some 10,000 prisoners did time at Port Arthur during its 47 years of operation.

As if that legacy of suffering wasn't enough, Port Arthur hit the headlines for the wrong reasons in 1996, when a maniacal visitor gunned down 53 men, women and children, killing 35, in the world's worst peacetime massacre; a memorial garden pays tribute. Admission price to Port Arthur includes a brief walking tour and a harbour cruise, leaving from the information centre. Boats run twice daily to the Isle of the Dead.

Wilderness

For many Australians from the other side of the Bass Strait, Tasmania is the closest they can get to European-style scenery. At such a distance from Europe, though, the landscape is almost untouched by civilisation. There is one good reason why it has remained unspoilt: it's often unapproachable by road. Four-wheel-drive vehicles, canoes, rafts or just sturdy legs are the best methods of penetrating these wild places. In Tasmania a higher percentage of the total area has been set aside as national parks than in any other state.

Even so, attempts by various commercial interests to log or dam unspoiled wilderness regions have triggered clashes with Tasmania's strong conservationist movement. According to the Wilderness Society of Tasmania, an average of 20,000 hectares (50,000 acres) of native forest is logged in the state each year, much of it in pure, 'old-growth' forest. The Society continues its campaign to save the state's remaining stands of old-growth forest available for logging.

The best known Wilderness Society campaign was the successful Franklin Blockade of 1982 which helped save the wild Franklin River from damming. Base for the campaigners was the West Coast fishing port of Strahan, which now derives its income from scenic cruises on the pristine Gordon River (into which the Franklin flows) and flights over the Franklin, which can also be experienced on gruelling four- to 10-day rafting trips. The West Coast Wilderness Railway (for bookings, tel: 1800 628 288), a redevelopment of a 19th-century line, now links Strahan to the nearby town of Queenstown, its surrounding hills laid bare by the effects of copper mining.

Cradle Mountain's jagged peak

South West National Park, covering most of the southwestern corner of Tasmania, has a variety of spectacular scenery, including rugged mountains, glacial lakes, icy rivers and forests of giant Antarctic beeches.

Cradle Mountain-Lake St Clair National Park is a few hours' drive northwest of Hobart. Here you'll find a wonderland carved out by glaciers: craggy mountain peaks, lakes and tarns, and extensive buttongrass plains. Extending through the length of the park, from the jagged grandeur of Cradle Mountain reflected in tranquil Dove Lake, south to the glacier-gouged deepwater basin of Lake St Clair, is the 80-km (50-mile) Overland Track, a wilderness walk that takes at least five days to complete. But it's not necessary to exert yourself: you can enjoy day walks and the breathtaking scenery from very comfortable lodges at Cradle Mountain or Lake St Clair.

WHAT TO DO

SPORT

Sporting life in Australia is inescapable, from the dawn jogger puffing past your window to the football crowds celebrating late into the night with shouting, songs and car horns. In a country so beautiful, and with a climate so benign, you'll be tempted to join the sporting crowds, either playing the game yourself or watching the professionals. Under the dependable sun, everything is possible, from skiing – on water or snow – to surfing to sailing.

Spectator sports are also a passion. You can measure their impact by the newspapers, with their comprehensive sports sections, and by the amount of live sports coverage and results on television and radio. If Australians are not playing a game or watching it, they're most likely betting on the result, or at least arguing about it.

In what other country could a racehorse be as revered as is Phar Lap, winner of the 1930 Melbourne Cup? When he died, after a heroic victory in the United States, flags flew at half-mast in Sydney. Today Phar Lap's body is the star attraction in Melbourne Museum, and his mighty heart is preserved at the National Museum of Australia in Canberra. The Melbourne Cup race itself brings the nation to a temporary halt as everyone tunes in to listen.

Sporting tastes have changed over time. More than a century ago, a guidebook gloomily reported that very little hunting was available around Sydney, except when 'occasionally parties are made up for rabbit, wallaby or kangaroo shooting'. In 1903 the first car race was run in Australia. Three years later surf bathing in the daytime became legal in Sydney. And waterskiing caught on in 1936. Australia won the

Davis Cup in 1939. When Melbourne hosted the Olympic Games in 1956, Aussie athletes seized 35 of the medals. The world was becoming aware of Australia as one of the foremost sporting powers, a nation of aggressive competitors who could become champions in fields as varied as tennis and swimming, cricket and golf, athletics and rugby.

In 1983, joyous delirium swept the nation when the yacht *Australia II* captured the America's Cup. At the 1996 Atlanta Olympics, Australia was more successful per head of population than any of the top 20 countries. In 2000, at the Sydney Olympics, Australia came fourth in the medal tally (after the US, Russia and China), and at the 2006 Melbourne Commonwealth Games athletes collected a record number of medals. Australia's achievements in out-performing countries like Germany, France, Britain and Japan is even more remarkable considering its population – just 20 million.

A racing crew with their surf boat at Leighton Beach, Perth

Watersports

Australia's endless coastline provides enough beaches, coves and ports to keep the nation in the swim all year round. If that isn't enough, there are lakes, rivers and swimming pools, both Olympic-size and backyard versions. Watersports of every variety are here for the taking.

Swimming in the Indian Ocean, the Tasman Sea, or the Coral Sea is the sort of sport you'll long remember. But the surf can be as dangerous as it is invigorating. Most of the popular beaches are delineated by flags showing where it's safe to swim. Beware of undertow or shifting currents and always obey the instructions of lifeguards. Sharks are a problem in some areas, with occasional attacks on bathers, and very occasional fatalities. When a shark alert is sounded, beat an immediate retreat to the shore and ask questions later.

Swimming amid the colourful fauna of the Great Barrier Reef

In spite of their mild-sounding name, box jellyfish are a serious seasonal danger, especially in the tropical north; elsewhere there may be Portuguese men-of-war, sea snakes or other silent menaces. Check locally before you even put a foot in the surf. A final word of caution: before you stretch out on the beach, make sure that you protect yourself from the sun, which is more powerful than you think. Light complexions are particularly vulnerable to quick, painful sunburn and worse.

Snorkelling brings you into intimate contact with a brilliant new world full of multicoloured fish and coral. The sport requires a minimum of equipment – a mask and breathing tube and, optionally, flippers to expand your range of operations. Practically anyone can learn how to snorkel in a matter of minutes, and there is no great skill or stamina required.

Scuba diving with an air tank is the advanced version of snorkelling. The best place in Australia for scuba outings – and quite possibly the best place in the world – is the coral wonderland of the Great Barrier Reef. Some of the resort islands are equipped for all the needs of divers, though you may have to supply your own regulator and demand valves. If you want to learn the sport, some resorts have weekly courses starting in the swimming pool or a quiet cove, and leading up to an Open Water Certificate. Elsewhere along Australia's coasts, some serious scuba divers devote themselves to exploring submerged wrecks.

Surfing. Yet another discovery by the intrepid Captain Cook, who came upon this sport in Hawaii. He wrote: 'The boldness and address with which we saw them perform these difficult and dangerous manoeuvres was altogether astonishing...' It was nearly two centuries before the first world championships were to be held in Sydney. Surfing areas are marked by signs, flags or discs. The best-known surfing zone in the country must be Sydney's Bondi Beach, but there are many other fine locations up and down the coast of New South Wales. Although Queensland's Surfers Paradise may be just that, many of the experts prefer the giant rollers

Surfing is a popular pastime along Australia's coasts

farther north at Noosa. Victoria's most popular surfing area is around Torquay. On the west coast, there are easily accessible surfing beaches close to Perth, Bunbury and Margaret River.

Sailing. Visiting yachts and their crews will always get a warm Aussie-style welcome. At popular resorts, for instance along the Gold Coast or the Great Barrier Reef, yachts and powerboats can be chartered, with or without a professional skipper. Inland, you can command a sailing boat or a houseboat on the relaxing Murray River. Or you might just want to settle for an hour's rental of a pedal boat.

Fishing. You'll need a licence to fish inland waters in some states, but the sea is free for all amateurs. Outstanding trout fishing is found in Tasmania and the Snowy Mountains. Seasons and bag limits vary with the district. As for game fishing, the challenge of the giant black marlin is best met off the northern coast of Queensland. If your catch weighs less than half a tonne, it's polite to throw the little fellow back. Or settle for tuna, mackerel or sailfish. Good deep-sea fishing is also found off the coast of Western Australia, especially at Geraldton, and in the Spencer Gulf, near Adelaide. In the north, a coveted game fish is the barramundi – a great fighter prized for its delicate flesh.

Sports Ashore

Golf. The landscaping may be foreign, the climate may be a better year-round bet than you're accustomed to, but the game's the same. Melbourne considers itself the nation's golfing capital, with championship courses such as Victoria and the Royal Melbourne. All the cities have golf clubs; they often operate under exchange agreements with clubs overseas, or you may have to be introduced by a local member. With no formality at all you can rent a set of clubs and play at one of the public courses to be found in all the sizeable towns. Golf is also a popular spectator sport in Australia. The Australian Open takes place in November.

Tennis. Having produced so many illustrious tennis champions, Australia takes the game seriously. You'll find courts available in the towns and resorts; some rent rackets and shoes. If you're just watching, then join the crowd. The world's top tennis stars usually tour Australia in December and January. Melbourne Park (formerly Flinders Park) hosts the Australian Open, one of tennis's four Grand Slam tournaments, in January every year.

Bushwalking (hiking). All over Australia there are numerous national parks boasting excellent walking tracks suitable for a wide range of abilities. If you are thinking of doing a long walk, make sure you have a map, good footwear, and adequate clothing and provisions (especially water). Wherever you go, always stay on the marked walking tracks.

Skiing. The season in the Australian Alps usually lasts from June to September, and on rare occasions into November, which should be inducement enough for skiers from the Northern Hemisphere. The best-known and best-equipped of the ski resorts in the Snowy Mountains, straddling the border of News South Wales and Victoria, include Thredbo Village, Perisher Valley and Smiggin Holes (NSW) and Mt Buller, Falls Creek, Mt Hotham and Mt Buffalo (Victoria).

Football and Rugby

In Australia the subject of football is so vast and complex – for a start, four different kinds of football are played – that the stranger is likely to be left gasping on the sidelines. But since the country is crazy about it, at least a few definitions may be useful. Incidentally, whatever type of football is being discussed, the fans are likely to call it 'footy'.

'Aussie Rules'

'Aussie Rules' was first played by Victoria gold miners in the 1850s, and the Melbourne Football Club was founded in 1858 – but the game's official rules were not established until 1866.

Australian Rules Football ('Aussie Rules') was first introduced in Melbourne in 1858, and although the Australian Football League (AFL) now includes teams in most major cities, the sport finds its most fanatical following in and around Melbourne. It is estimated that, every winter Saturday in the city, one person in 16 attends an AFL game, and thousands more follow the saturation TV coverage. The Grand Final, held at the Melbourne Cricket Ground in September, is one of the world's great sporting experiences, rivalling an English FA Cup Final or an American Super Bowl for colour, passion and atmosphere.

The sport, which combines elements of rugby, Gaelic football and other forms of the game, is characterised by long-distance kicks and passes and high scoring on an oversized but crowded field – with 18 players to a side. The game is divided into four 25-minute quarters.

Rugby League started as a 13-man alternative to Rugby Union, and is played today nationally through the National Rugby League (NRL) competition, although the sport's heartland is in Sydney, Brisbane and Canberra. It's a rough-house game, physical rather than cerebral, based on an uncompromising masochistic style of defence that prompted one American football coach to observe: 'Our guys could never stand up to that sort of constant punishment.' League attendances are nothing like as large as those of the AFL, but the Sydney clubs – such as St George Illawarra Dragons, Penrith Panthers, Manly Sea Eagles and Parramatta Eels – keep their star players fabulously well paid through TV rights deals and revenue from their licensed clubs. The Aussie national side, known as the Kangaroos, regularly hops through tours of France and Great Britain unbeaten.

A Sydney AFL supporter

Rugby Union, the 15-a-side, formerly amateur version of the game, is fast, rough and engrossing to the fans. Compared with Rugby League, the game traditionally had a 'silvertail' (upper-crust) image based partly on its strength in the universities and private schools. Now that Union is fully professional, the gentlemanly spirit is less in evidence. Since 1995, teams representing Queensland, New South Wales and the Australian Capital Territory have competed every winter in the Super 12 tournament, against sides from New Zealand and South Africa. The Australian national team, the Wallabies, regularly takes on its two Southern Hemisphere rivals in the Tri-Nations competition.

Soccer is the oldest of the country's football games but, compared with the three other species, is the poor relation. It kicked off in the 19th century among earnest British migrants, more or less stagnated until after World War II, then was revitalised by the arrival of immigrants from southern Europe. Today most clubs in the A-League are dominated by players from the Italian, Greek, Croatian, Slavic, Maltese, Dutch and Macedonian communities. The Australian national team is called the Socceroos.

Australian Champions

Australia has bred many world-class winners. Below are some of the pre-eminent sporting personalities of the 20th and 21st centuries:

Athletics
- Herb Elliott
- Ron Clarke
- Robert DeCastella
- Cathy Freeman

Motor racing
- Jack Brabham
- Alan Jones
- Peter Brock

Cricket
- Don Bradman
- Greg Chappell
- Dennis Lillee

- Ricky Ponting
- Shane Warne

Golf
- Peter Thompson
- Greg Norman
- Stuart Appleby
- Ian Baker-Finch
- Wayne Grady

Swimming
- Dawn Fraser
- Samantha Riley
- Kieren Perkins
- Grant Hackett

- Ian Thorpe
- Michael Klim
- Susan O'Neill

Tennis
- Evonne Goolagong
- Margaret Court
- Rod Laver
- Pat Cash
- Pat Rafter
- Lleyton Hewitt
- The 'Woodies' (Mark Woodforde, Todd Woodbridge)

Other Spectator Sports

The Australians have been playing **cricket** since the early days of the penal colony at Sydney Cove. In its traditional form, the game can go on for five days, and even then it may finish in a draw. It was the Australian media mogul Kerry Packer who had the temerity to make a show-biz spectacle out of a gentlemanly pursuit, staging games at night under floodlights, in gaudy uniforms, and ending the match

Cricket has a loyal following

decisively in a single day. Fortunately for conservative fans, the old-fashioned Test survives as well under the Australian sun, and the current Aussie team is recognised as the strongest in the world at the five-day game. The season extends from October to the end of March, with matches played at interstate level (the Sheffield Shield), down through district ranks to the junior and social levels.

Horseracing. Practically every Australian town, even in the Outback, has a racecourse, and the big cities tend to have more than one. The best times to go to the races are Saturdays and holidays. Betting on horses, or most other things, is as Australian as ice-cold beer. Enthusiasts who can't make it to the course can participate in their own way through off-track betting facilities, legal and computerised and called TAB for Totalisator Agency Board. For punters who prefer to patronise illegal bookmakers, they are seldom far away.

The biggest competition of the year in the Australian horse-racing season is the Melbourne Cup, a two-mile classic

Birdsville Races

Every September in the remote Queensland Outback town of Birdsville, the Birdsville Picnic Races attract enormous crowds. The population of Birdsville leaps from 30 to 3,000 overnight, with many spectators arriving by light planes from all over Australia.

that is followed so obsessively that the day it is run – the first Tuesday in November – is a public holiday in Victoria. Even the process of government is suspended so that the nation's decision-makers in Canberra can watch the live telecast.

Trotting (harness racing) can be seen in big cities and some provincial locations. In the capital cities the trotters run at night under floodlights.

Greyhound racing is another spectacle that draws crowds of punters. The dogs usually run in the cool of the evening; the audiences at the track can be as fascinating as the sport itself.

Motor racing. Big races take place near Brisbane, Sydney and Melbourne. The biggest of all is the Australian Formula 1 Grand Prix in Melbourne, where you can watch the world championship contenders compete.

ENTERTAINMENT

Australia receives the best the world can offer in the performing arts, as well as producing masterpieces of its own. Open any major city newspaper for advertised performances of chamber music, opera, avant-garde plays, Aboriginal theatre, comedy, cabaret, Shakespearean classics, rock concerts, Broadway hits, dance, art shows and touring exhibitions from the top galleries of Europe and North America.

Australia's two largest cities, Sydney and Melbourne, present the greatest number of cultural events, although Adelaide, in South Australia, plays hosts to one of the most

Bangarra Dance Theatre blends Aboriginal and Western styles

extensive and exciting arts festivals – the Adelaide Festival, held biennially in even-numbered years.

Throughout the country, a lot of racy entertainment can be seen, as well as higher-brow cultural attractions such as opera, ballet, concerts and drama. Between the extremes there's a whole range of entertainment options for a good evening out.

In some smaller towns, odd events such as cane-toad racing, thong throwing (an open-toed sandal is hurled as far as possible) and brick-throwing draw the crowds. In coastal towns and cities, summer surf carnivals are another favourite – a chance for lifeguards to show off their skills, as well as a celebration of Australian beach culture.

On Stage

Theatre has been going strong in Australia for a couple of centuries. In 1789, scarcely a year after New South Wales was founded, a troupe of convicts in Sydney put on a Restoration comedy *(The Recruiting Officer)* by George Farquhar as part of the celebrations for the birthday of King George III. The Theatre Royal, built in Hobart in 1834, is Australia's oldest. Sir Laurence Olivier described it as 'the best little theatre in the world'. Drama today is at its liveliest in Sydney and Melbourne but you can enjoy performances in most cities.

Opera has attracted keen audiences Down Under since the days of Dame Nellie Melba. In more recent times, the coloratura brilliance of Dame Joan Sutherland spread her fame around the world. Grand opera in the Sydney Opera House is a gala occasion; but opera-goers in other cities may enjoy better acoustics and atmosphere in their newer theatres.

On the decks in Brisbane

Ballet and dance. The country's leading classical dance company, the Australian Ballet, founded in 1962, is based in Melbourne but performs in Sydney as well. Leading modern dance troupes include the Sydney Dance Company, the Australian Dance Theatre and the Bangarra Dance Theatre. All varieties of dance have a following, from ballroom dancing (as seen in the Australian movie *Strictly Ballroom*) to tap-dancing (as depicted in the Australian film *Bootmen*).

Music

Every state and territory in Australia has its own symphony orchestra; many maintain youth and chamber orchestras as well. An influential promoter of serious music, Musica Viva Australia, presents thousands of concerts each year across the country. Sydney holds free – and hugely popular – open-air opera and classical concerts each year in the Domain as part of the Sydney Festival.

Jazz clubs exist in all the big cities, where you might hear a visiting celebrity or an up-and-coming local band. Plenty of pubs feature jazz, but usually at weekends only. Both indoor and outdoor jazz concerts are also advertised.

Other music – pop, rock, folk or rap – can reveal something of a nation's soul. Aussie options range from a bearded troubadour dishing out bush ballads in an Outback saloon to hard-hitting metal bands. Contemporary groups such as Silverchair, Powderfinger and The Vines follow in the wake of past notables like the Seekers, the Bee Gees, Men at Work, INXS, Midnight Oil, AC/DC and Cold Chisel.

Nightlife

The scale and sophistication of an evening's entertainment depends on the size of the town. You won't find Jennifer Lopez or Sir Elton John performing in Burrumbuttock, New South Wales, but nightlife in Australia's smaller towns and remoter areas can still be a load of fun, as anyone who has attended an Outback bush dance or seen that wacky Australian movie *The Adventures of Priscilla, Queen of the Desert* will know.

In larger centres and cities, nightlife venues, acts and attractions are listed in guides published in the daily newspapers, usually on Thursdays or Fridays. Posters slapped on walls and telegraph poles proclaim dance parties, gigs, plays and concerts. Music pubs and private clubs provide more mainstream entertainment; it's usually quite easy for non-members to enter the latter.

Clubs subsidise their meals and entertainment with profits from their slot machines, called poker machines (more affectionately, pokies). For punters who prefer to wager serious money, gambling **casinos** are available in big cities and resorts. Usually open very late into the night, casinos are typically equipped for, among other pursuits: roulette, craps, keno, blackjack, baccarat and the backwoods game of two-up in a more refined, electronic version.

Cinema

Nicole Kidman and Cate Blanchett are probably Australia's best-known contemporary film stars. Other cinematic high fliers include Geoffrey Rush (winner of the 1997 best actor Oscar for *Shine*), Naomi Watts, Hugh Jackman and the great swashbuckler Errol Flynn, who hailed from Tasmania. New Zealand-born Russell Crowe – who won the 2001 best actor Oscar for *Gladiator* – lives in Australia.

Founded at the end of the 19th century, the Australian film industry took a great leap forward in the 1970s and has never really looked back. Films such as *Picnic at Hanging Rock*, *My Brilliant Career*, *Breaker Morant*, the *Mad Max* series and *Crocodile Dundee* – as well as the more off-beat *Strictly Ballroom*, *Muriel's Wedding* and *The Adventures of Priscilla, Queen of the Desert* – have given audiences around the world a glimpse of Australia's scenery and perhaps provided insight into the national character and preoccupations. More recently *The Dish*, *Rabbit-Proof Fence* and *Wolf Creek* have also excelled. Multi-screen cinema complexes are popular in town centres as well as suburbs. Big cities also have specialised cinemas showing art films, foreign films and revivals. The Sydney Film Festival in June showcases the best new films selected from recent film festivals around the world.

An upmarket shopping in Melbourne's GPO mall

SHOPPING

In most cities, the browsers and window-shoppers congregate along the pedestrian malls. Department-store chains David Jones and Myer provide a dependable cross-section of what's available. Downtown arcades and courts have smaller boutiques handling everything from high fashion to silly souvenirs.

In Sydney the skyscrapers have subterranean shopping arcades; the Queen Victoria Building by Town Hall station is a great place to browse. In Melbourne the main shopping streets are Collins and Bourke, along with Bourke Street Mall. Rundle Mall is the essence of shopping in Adelaide, and traffic-free Hay Street Mall is Perth's equivalent.

The state capitals are home to one or more general **markets**, where stall-holders sell everything from clothing, jewellery and craftware to paintings, antiques and books. They are usually staged at weekends. Three prominent examples are

Sydney's Paddington Markets, Hobart's Salamanca Market and Darwin's Mindil Beach Sunset Markets – each with its own distinctive goods and atmosphere. If you are visiting country towns, keep an eye out for notices advertising markets. These can be great places to absorb local atmosphere, find unusual offerings, and, perhaps, pick up a bargain.

Shopping hours usually run nonstop from 8.30 or 9am to 5 or 5.30pm, Monday to Friday, and to 5pm on Saturdays in major towns and cities. One night a week, either Thursday or Friday depending on the city, stores stay open until 9pm or thereabouts. In larger cities, tourist needs are catered for on Sundays as well.

Elaborately painted didgeridoos for sale in Cairns

While shopping, keep in mind that overseas visitors are allowed to claim back the 10 percent GST (goods and services tax) added to all purchases (*see page 247*).

Aboriginal Arts and Crafts

Some good places to find authentic boomerangs, didgeridoos and works of art are the Northern Territory and North Queensland, but you can find Aboriginal products in speciality stores all over the country. Outback artists produce traditional paintings on bark, the subjects and style recalling the prehistoric rock paintings featuring kangaroos, emus, fish, snakes, crocodiles and impressions of tribal ceremonies. Other indigenous painters use modern materials to produce canvases in a style that looks uncannily like some abstract-expressionist work, yet recounting Dreamtime legends and rituals. Though the themes are old, the economics are contemporary: the price tags on paintings may go into four or even five figures.

Fine workmanship is also seen on some of the painted wood sculptures of animals and birds. You'll see large, brightly decorated didgeridoos – wind instruments made from tree trunks hollowed out by obliging termites. Slightly easier to transport are clap-sticks for percussion accompaniment. Some Aboriginal craftsmen also produce decorated wooden shields and, rather inevitably, boomerangs. Baskets and table-mats woven from pandanus leaves are perhaps easier to carry home.

A word of warning: fakes and kitsch are sometimes represented as Aboriginal art by unscrupulous traders. To help identify genuine Aboriginal and Torres Strait Islander art, cultural products and services, Aboriginal communities have developed the Label of Authenticity, which employs the Aboriginal colours black, red and yellow and is protected by law.

Art and Antiques

Paintings and prints by contemporary Australian artists are on show in commercial galleries in many areas, but the biggest concentration is in the big cities. Sydney galleries are clustered in the central shopping district and in Paddington. In Melbourne visit the City, Toorak Road and High Street, Armadale. They'll handle the packing, insurance and shipping details for you.

Antiques include some worthy colonial pieces: furniture, clocks, jewellery, porcelain, silverware, glassware and maps. Some dealers specialise in non-Australian antiques, for instance Chinese ceramics or Japanese screens. In Sydney, the Woollahra district is full of antiques shops. Melbourne's antiques centre is High Street, Armadale.

Huon pine, a slow-growing conifer unique to Tasmania, has long attracted the attention of wood-carvers. The timber, which is heavy, fine-grained and perfumed, is carved into furniture, salad bowls, egg-cups, candlesticks and even hair-curlers. If there's no room for a carved artefact in your luggage, you can buy sachets of sweet-scented Huon pine shavings, to breathe in when you feel nostalgic for Tassie.

Clothing

The **fashion** season just ending in Australia is always about to begin north of the equator – so Australian end-of-season sales can deliver excellent bargains that are instantly wearable upon your return home. 'Wearable art' in swimwear, fashion garments, fabrics and souvenirs proliferates. Names to look for include Ken Done, Leona Edmiston, Balarinji Australia, Country Road, Covers, Trent Nathan, Saba, Lisa Ho, Hussy, Studibaker Hawk, Perri Cutten, Von Troska, Alannah Hill, Trelise Cooper, Scanlan & Theodore, Morrissey, Collette Dinnigan, Zimmerman Wear and Carla Zampatti.

A distinct style of **Outback clothing** has evolved from rural Australia, the area collectively known as 'The Bush'. Driza-bone oilskin raincoats, Akubra hats (wide-brimmed hats that are usually made of felt) and the R.M. Williams range of bush wear (including boots and moleskin trousers) are good examples. Consider buying a pair of Blundstone boots, designed in Tasmania and renowned for their durability.

Museum shops

Australia's major museums all have gift shops, and many of them sell specially commissioned items, such as reproduction artworks or Aboriginal artefacts, that cannot be bought elsewhere.

Sheepskin. In a country where sheep outnumber people by seven to one, sheep products are put to good use. Their hides are manufactured into a wide range of items. If it isn't too hot to think about it, you can choose from sheepskin boots, hats, coats, rugs and novelty items.

Woollen goods. It's those sheep again. Look for high-quality sweaters and scarves, and tapestries, too. You can also buy hand-spun wool. Australian merino sheep produce fine fleece ideally suited for spinning. All kinds of knitwear, from vivid children's clothing to Jumbuk brand greasy wool sweaters (which retain their natural water resistance) are available.

An old-fashioned arcade

Precious Stones

Australia is the source of about 95 percent of the world's **opals**. 'White' opals are mined from the fields of Andamooka and Coober Pedy in South Australia, where inhabitants live underground to escape searing summer heat. 'Boulder' opals – bright and vibrant – come from Quilpie in Queensland, while the precious 'black' opal (actually more blue than black) is mined at Lightning Ridge and White Cliffs in New South Wales. Opals, considered among Australia's best buys, are sold unset or as finished jewellery. Larger jewellery shops can arrange duty-free purchase for

Fine opals on sale in Sydney

foreign visitors, but you may have to pay duty when you arrive home. The products are virtually unrivalled anywhere else in the world.

After opals, **sapphires** are Australia's most-mined gemstones. A sapphire is exactly the same stone as a ruby – the only difference is the name and the colour. Creative Australian jewellers work wonders with sapphires.

Diamonds are mined by Argyle Diamond Mines in the rugged Kimberley region in the country's northwest; Australia is one of the world's largest diamond sources. The Kimberley is famed for its 'pink' diamonds, sometimes marketed under the description 'champagne'. Hues range from lightly flushed to deep red.

Souvenirs

Souvenirs, whether ingenious or hackneyed, indigenous or imported, pop up everywhere you travel: in cities, resorts and along the way at roadside stands. Tourists seem unable to resist miniature kangaroos, koalas and, in Tasmania, almost-lovable Tasmanian devil dolls.

A selection of plastic boomerangs and beer can-holders head the very long list of less artistic souvenirs, followed by saucy T-shirts. In Sydney, you'll find them cheap at Paddy's Market. In Melbourne, try Queen Victoria Market.

Kangaroo-skin souvenirs include toy kangaroos and koalas and other such products – some of them quite trite. The cheapest of them, often wrapped up in patriotic Australian packaging, are imported.

Calendar of Events

January

Sydney Festival: a month of music, dance, theatre and the visual arts.

Perth Cup: horse racing classic at Royal Ascot Racecourse.

Country Music Festival, Tamworth, New South Wales.

Australian Tennis Open: Grand Slam event at Melbourne Park.

Hobart Summer Festival: two-week celebration of culture and food, beginning late December.

Port Lincoln Tunarama Festival: on the foreshore of Boston Bay, South Australia (includes the world tuna-throwing championships).

February

Sydney Gay and Lesbian Mardi Gras Parade: fun-filled, provocative parade along Oxford Street.

Perth Festival: sporting and cultural events.

Adelaide Festival of Arts (even-numbered years): three weeks of opera, ballet, theatre, art and literary events.

Launceston Cup: the social event of Tasmania. Much more than just a horse race, it is the culmination of a one-month racing programme.

March–April

Australian Grand Prix: Formula 1 racing at Albert Park, Melbourne.

Moomba Waterfest, Melbourne: carnival with fireworks, music, river pageants and a street parade.

Canberra National Multicultural Festival.

Womadelaide: Australian and international artists take part in this world music festival held in Adelaide.

South Australia Vintage Festival, Barossa Valley (odd-numbered years): celebrating the wine harvest with German-Australian gaiety.

Sydney Royal Easter Show, at Olympic Park.

Sydney Cup Week: a pageant of horse racing.

May

Barossa Valley Balloon Regatta: Nuriootpa in the Barossa Valley.

Adelaide Cup: horse race and associated festivities.

Australian Celtic Festival, New South Wales: dancing, singing and art.

June

Sydney Film Festival.

Darwin Beer Can Regatta: all the boats constructed of used beer cans.

A Taste of Manly: annual food and wine festival.

Bounty Day, Norfolk Island: 8 June (anniversary of the *Bounty* mutineers' arrival in 1856), festivities culminate in a Bounty Ball.

Brisbane Cup: horse race.

July

Camel Cup: camel racing at Blatherskite Park, Alice Springs.

Gold Coast Marathon: Queensland.

Melbourne Grand National: steeplechase.

Royal Darwin Show: agricultural exhibition.

August–September

Royal Queensland Show, Brisbane: agricultural fair with fireworks.

Mount Isa Rodeo and Festival, Queensland: Australia's biggest rodeo.

Henley-on-Todd Regatta, Alice Springs: dry-land bottomless boat race.

Australian Masters Alpine Ski Races: Snowy Mountains.

Royal Adelaide Show: South Australia's agricultural summit meeting.

Royal Melbourne Show: bucolic and sporting attractions.

Carnival of Flowers: Toowoomba, Queensland.

Birdsville Races, Queensland: a weekend of horse racing and revelry.

Floriade, Canberra: Australia's biggest flower show.

Jabiru Wind Festival: cultural community event in Kakadu National Park.

Australian Motorcycle Grand Prix: Phillip Island, Victoria.

October

Melbourne International Arts Festival: visual and performing arts.

Royal Hobart Agricultural Show: Tasmania's agricultural highlight.

Sydney Sleaze Ball: themed gay and lesbian party.

November

Melbourne Cup: one of the world's premier horse-racing events.

December

Western Australian Turf Club Derby: horse racing.

Sydney–Hobart: one of the world's toughest yacht races.

Various capital cities: New Year's Eve celebrations with fireworks.

EATING OUT

If you enjoy dining out at down-to-earth prices, with a wide choice of menus reflecting varied ethnic influences, you're going to enjoy mealtimes in Australia's cities. Eating well in the land down under doesn't carry an inflated price tag. The whole country is well stocked with inexpensive bistros, cafés and food markets where diverse and wholesome cuisine can be enjoyed at moderate prices.

All state capitals have a lively café and restaurant scene in their inner-city areas. Most restaurants support 'BYO' ('bring your own'), allowing you to take along store-bought wine to enjoy with your meal (a small 'corkage' charge usually applies). Australian wine is relatively inexpensive and of high quality – you can buy it at pubs or from a wide variety of liquor outlets (although not from supermarkets in most states). Many other restaurants are licensed, with their own wine cellars (some licensed restaurants also allow you to BYO, but check first).

The average urban-dwelling Australian may eat out two or three times a week – a testimony to the quality and affordability of the food. In the words of Barbara Kafka, one of America's foremost food writers and cookbook authors, 'Australians have one of the most extraordinary assortments of basic ingredients of high quality anywhere in the world, and at exceptionally modest prices.'

Australian cooks have the advantage of the availability

Delicious waffles

of a wonderful palette of ingredients. The country's climatic diversity provides a wide range of fresh vegetables and fruits, ranging from exotic rambutans, coconuts and lychees to apples, pears and spinach.

This culinary wonderland has developed gradually over the last three decades. During most of the two centuries of modern Australia's existence, its inhabitants subsisted on bland 'meat and veg' fodder, in which lamb chops and three vegetables were standard fare. Cultural intermingling since World War II has revolutionised the national diet. Urban Australia now eats what has been described as 'fusion food' – a collage of culinary influences, embracing European and

Indigenous Cuisine

Recent innovations by Australian chefs have included greater use of indigenous foods in fine dining. Lemon aspen, bush tomatoes, Illawarra plums, lemon myrtle, lilli pillies, muntari berries and other mysterious ingredients are now appearing on menus, often blended with traditional dishes of meat and fish. Kangaroo and emu are commercially farmed and processed. (Both meats are low in fat and high in protein.) Collectively known as native food – or sometimes bush tucker – these are just some of the fruits, seeds, nuts, fungi, mammals, reptiles, fish and birds that sustained Australia's indigenous inhabitants for up to 100,000 years before white settlers came to the region.

Other bush-tucker ingredients include quandongs (similar to a peach with a touch of rhubarb), wattle seeds (sometimes used in ice cream), Kakadu plums (less sweet than the usual variety) and bunya bunya nuts (delicious in satay). Even wilder Aboriginal ingredients, very rarely seen in restaurants, include the Bogong moth (a hefty moth roasted in a fire and eaten like a peanut) and the witchetty grub (a puffy, white grub found in the trunks and roots of certain wattle trees), which has been shown to be a virtual powerhouse of protein.

Asian influences, that enlivens basic fish, grain or meat with, for example, a handful of chopped coriander, a splash of olive oil and a dash of chilli.

If you're into exotic fare, sample goat cheeses from Western Australia or Victoria, cold-pressed olive oils from South Australia, buffalo mozzarella from New South Wales, barramundi fish from the Northern Ter-

Seafood-lovers are spoilt for choice in Australia

ritory, or oysters, scallops, salmon and other seafood ingredients from Tasmania's waters.

Fine-dining options are generally restricted to inner-city areas and some wine-producing regions, but most suburbs and country towns have at least one decent Thai or Chinese restaurant. There are, however, culinary blackholes, especially in remote rural areas, where café menus will probably include nothing more exotic than spaghetti bolognese. The traditional Aussie meat pie, doused liberally with tomato sauce, rules supreme in these outposts, as does the hamburger. Outside the standardised US chains, Australian hamburgers tend to include beetroot and lettuce rather than pickle.

What to Eat

Breakfast is anything you want it to be, from muesli and grapes or coffee and croissant to a full cooked meal. It depends on where you are and your hunger level. If you are really starving, some establishments will serve you a breakfast based on steak or lamb chops with eggs. It's also possible to find original oddities such as tinned spaghetti on toast.

Fish and seafood. From traditional fish and chips eaten standing up to lobster savoured by candlelight, Australia's temperate and tropical oceans offer a fantastic choice of seafood. Fish adorning the menu include the delicious snapper, the meaty John Dory, smallish flounder and bigger sole, the bony but flavoursome whiting (no relation to the English whiting) and the tropical trevally. Then there's barramundi, which means 'big scales' in an Aboriginal language, and is found in both fresh and salt water; game fishermen in the north take 'barra' of up to 15kg (33lb). Along the Great Barrier Reef they even eat red emperor, a fish so gorgeous it might take a snorkeller's breath away.

Treat yourself to succulent seafood specialities such as Sydney rock oysters, as delicious as any in the world, and Brisbane's famous Moreton Bay bug, a crustacean to gloat over, and gloriously meaty mud crabs. Lobster, grilled or thermidor, is priced for special occasions. You are also likely to come across some of the lobster's freshwater cousins, small crayfish known locally as yabbies. Prices are less forbidding when it comes to steamed mussels or prawns. A popular and simple Australian alfresco meal for two consists of a kilo (2.2lb) of prawns and a bottle of ice-cold white wine. Scrumptious!

Meat favourites include steak and roast lamb, particularly in simpler restaurants, and pork is also popular. Good-quality organic meats are now on offer at many city and country restaurants. Meat pies are a long-established staple; in Adelaide the speciality is the 'floater', a pie served floating in pea soup. If you're feeling adventurous, you can even dine on some Australian native fauna, such as kangaroo, crocodile or emu; all three are usually served rare.

Vegetables are available in as much variety as anywhere else in the world. As with meat, organic vegetables are on the rise. In restaurants, either vegetables or a salad may accompany your main course, but note that there is a trend for city restaurants to charge extra for these 'sides'.

Fruit in Australia covers all the climatic zones. To name a few: the more familiar apples, cherries, plums and berries from the temperate latitudes; and tropical avocados, bananas, papayas, passion fruit, pineapples and mangoes.

Desserts. You'll be able to find as many as you might want, from light fruit-based offerings to heavy puddings. A traditional Australian favourite is the light and fluffy pavlova, a meringue concoction traditionally topped with kiwi fruit. It's a little unfashionable these days, but worth sampling if you can get it. Peach Melba, created for Melbourne's most famous opera singer Nellie Melba by the great chef Escoffier, is still sometimes found on dessert menus. Also look for ice cream flavoured with wattle seed – roasted ground acacia seeds – which tastes a bit like coffee.

Dining outdoors in Perth

Exotic Imports

The massive migration from Mediterranean countries – mainly Italy and Greece – after World War II made the first real dent in Australia's monolithic Anglo-Saxon palate. Italians in particular helped revolutionise cooking, introducing wary Aussies to the wonders of pasta, garlic and olive oil. Today, each capital city has its concentration of Italian restaurants – Melbourne's Lygon Street in the suburb of Carlton and Sydney's Norton Street in Leichhardt being the most famous – serving authentic, well-priced food. In Melbourne, with its large Greek population, it is easy to find traditionally made *taramasalata*, *dolmades* or *souvlaki*.

Wine tasting

That was only the beginning. The extension of immigration in the 1970s added myriad new cuisines. The great melting-pot of Australian society meant that restaurants were suddenly opened by Lebanese, Turkish, Balkan, Hungarian and Spanish chefs.

The biggest recent influence has come from Asia. Regional Chinese, Thai, Vietnamese, Japanese and Indian restaurants are now Australia's biggest success stories, with Korean, Sri Lankan, Singaporean and Indonesian cuisines waiting in the wings. Every capital city offers *teppanyaki* dining rooms and take-away *laksa* stalls. Singapore-style 'food courts' have sprung up, which have several fast-food stalls offering meals from different Asian cuisines. Supermarkets stock the required pastes and condiments for everyone's favourite Thai or Indian dish.

Australian Wines

The wines of Australia are among the world's best – a judgment confirmed consistently at international wine shows. Not only are the country's finest wines world-beaters, but even the humble

A local red – the perfect accompaniment to a good meal

'kangarouge' sold in boxes ('casks') is the worthy equivalent of any *vin de table* served in a bistro in France. Australians drink more than twice as much wine per capita as Americans, and anything that's left over (800 million litres of it) is exported to over 100 countries. Wine is one of the country's most important export industries and the range sold in liquor stores is extensive and moderately priced.

Australia's interest in wine production stretches back a couple of centuries. The founder of the New South Wales colony, Captain Arthur Phillip, certainly had his priorities right, and one of the first projects he ordered in 1788 was the planting of vines at Sydney Cove. Because of factors such as the damp and the sea breezes, the site (now part of Sydney's Botanic Gardens) was quite wrong for growing grapes, which developed 'black spot', and the experiment failed. But in 1791 three acres of vines were successfully planted a few miles inland.

Rum, rather than wine, became the favourite drink under Governor Phillip's successor. Free-enterprising army officers enjoyed a monopoly on the staggeringly profitable sales of rum, and widespread abuses were reported to London. It was Captain William Bligh, the original hardliner of *Bounty* fame, who was dispatched to clean up Australia. Governor Bligh was deposed in the Rum Rebellion of 1808, a mutiny led by one of the first wine-growers, John Macarthur.

Today, most of Australia's European grape varieties are grown by some 7,800 vineyards on 158,000 hectares (390,000 acres) of vineyards. Riesling, Chardonnay and Semillon are the most favoured white varieties, while popular reds include Cabernet Sauvignon, Pinot Noir and Shiraz (also known in Europe as Syrah). Climatic conditions ranging from warm to hot provide excellent ripening, with an abundance of flavour and comparatively high alcohol levels. Australia's vintage (harvest) occurs between January and May each year.

Wine is produced in every state. The biggest producer is South Australia, where the best-known wineries are situated in the beautiful Barossa Valley, famed for its Shiraz. The most important wine-producing region of New South Wales is the Hunter Valley, noted for its Semillon and Shiraz. Victoria boasts numerous wine-growing regions (the Yarra Valley and Mornington Peninsula are the closest to Melbourne and specialise in cool-climate varieties), and Western Australia's Swan Valley and Margaret River areas have also made their mark with excellent Cabernets and Chardonnays. Tasmania's temperate climate produces some fine Pinot Noir.

If you're interested in seeing where the wine comes from, every state capital has wine-growing areas nearby, and the chance to sample wines at the cellar door is one of their most interesting features. As most wineries are concentrated in a relatively small area, they make ideal touring for a day or – better still – two days, either independently or on a guided tour.

The Amber Nectar

During the 19th century, most Australian beer was made like English ales, until, just over 100 years ago, German immigrants began to brew lighter Continental-style lagers in Melbourne. Nowadays lager is the dominant style, and it's hugely popular throughout the country.

Beer in Australia is served very cold. Low temperature is considered so important that beer-lovers will insist on glasses that have been chilled, or will keep their 'tinnie' (beer can) in an insulating jacket.

The best-known beer is probably Fosters lager, but that's only one of many va-

Downing a cold beer

rieties. Reschs, Tooheys, Victoria Bitter, Castlemaine XXXX, Swan, Cascade and Boags are also popular brands. Some beers are sold in 'new' and 'old' types, the first being lager and the latter darker in colour. Coopers beer, made in South Australia, is a favourite among connoisseurs – it's rich and strong, similar to the best British real ales.

Australia's standard alcoholic strength for canned beer is 4.9 percent – pretty strong by international standards. A word of advice for weight-watchers from Europe or America: the word 'light' or 'lite' applied to beer in Australia means lighter in alcohol, not lighter in calories. It has exactly the same calorific content as the regular type. The alcoholic strength of beer is displayed on the can or bottle.

HANDY TRAVEL TIPS

An A–Z Summary of Practical Information

A

ACCOMMODATION (see also CAMPING, YOUTH HOSTELS)

Australia welcomes the traveller with all kinds of accommodation. The luxury end of the spectrum matches the most sumptuous world standards, in the rooms and suites as well as the associated restaurants, lounges, saunas and spas. But even in budget-priced hotel and motel rooms you can expect a private shower or bath and toilet, a telephone, a TV set, a small refrigerator and coffee and tea-making equipment (and free coffee, tea and milk). In most regions, air-conditioning, or at least a ceiling fan, is provided.

There's no limit to the level of luxury a hotel or motel can attain, and either type can be anywhere – along the highway or right downtown. Distinguishing between the two can be confusing. The only sure difference is that a hotel has a bar open to the public – indeed, the most modest ones have little else to offer. To add to the confusion, 'hotel' is also a synonym for 'pub' here. If a motel has a bar, it's usually strictly for the guests. You simply can't judge a hostelry by what it calls itself.

Private hotels, often small guesthouses, do not have a licence for alcohol. Bed-and-breakfast establishments – private homes taking paying guests – exist in towns or out on the farms. Big towns and resorts also have self-catering apartments with maid service and fully equipped kitchens, convenient for longer stays.

Overseas offices of Tourism Australia have listings of hotels and motels – see <www.australia.com>. You can reserve accommodation through your travel agent, the nearest offices of the international and Australian hotel chains, or your airline. Within Australia, the state tourist bureaux, domestic airlines and hotel chains offer instant free bookings. If you arrive out of the blue, local tourist offices have desks for last-minute reservations.

Accommodation may be hard to find when Australians themselves go travelling en masse, during school holidays. These can vary, but most states have adopted a four-term school year with two-week breaks in April, June/July and September/October. The Christmas/summer holidays are from mid-December to the beginning of February.

AIRPORTS

The principal gateways are Sydney, Melbourne, Brisbane, Darwin and Perth. Other international airports serve Adelaide, Townsville, Hobart and Cairns. The domestic air network is very well developed, and even smallish towns usually have comfortable, efficient terminals. The biggest airports have the full range of restaurants and bars, newsstands, souvenir shops, post office and banks. The international airports have duty-free shops for both arriving and departing passengers.

Arriving passengers can travel from airport to town by taxi or bus. In Sydney, Brisbane, Adelaide, Darwin and Perth, airport bus services go to and from the door of most hotels. Travel time ranges from 20 minutes (Perth and Darwin) to 40 minutes (Sydney). Note that Sydney Airport's domestic and international terminals are a shuttle-bus ride apart. There's also a rail link between Sydney Airport and Central Station (<www.airportlink.com.au>).

Check-in time for departing passengers on domestic flights is one hour before the scheduled flight time; international flights require check-in at least two hours in advance.

B

BICYCLE HIRE

Most Australian cities are reasonably attuned to cyclists, and bicycle lanes are sometimes marked on inner-city streets. Cycling in Canberra is excellent, and the flatness of Melbourne and Adelaide make those cities popular with cyclists. Cars clog most large cities, however, and attempts to cater for cyclists are often little more than cosmetic. Throughout Australia, by law cyclists must wear helmets at all times.

Organised cycle tours of varying lengths are available, including transport to and from a scenic area (bikes provided), food and accommodation (Tasmania is a popular bike-touring destination). You can also rent touring bikes. For details, look up 'Bicycles & Accessories – Retail & Repairs' in the Yellow Pages phone book of the relevant city. Local cycling organisations are a good source of information:

Bicycle Federation of Australia: tel: (02) 6249 6761; <www.bfa.asn.au>.

Pedal Power ACT (Canberra): tel: (02) 6248 7995; <www.pedalpower.org.au>.

Bicycle New South Wales: tel: (02) 9218 5400; <www.bicyclensw.org.au>.

Bicycle Queensland: tel: (07) 3844 1144; <www.bq.org.au>.

Bicycle South Australia: tel: (08) 8232 2644; <www.bikesa.au>.

Bicycle Tasmania: tel: (03) 6266 4582; <www.biketas.org.au>.

Bicycle Victoria: tel: (03) 8636 8888; <www.bv.com.au>.

BUDGETING FOR YOUR TRIP

You can eat out well for little money: a plate of noodles or pasta can cost A$15 or less. Accommodation also represents good value when measured against equivalents in other developed countries. As far as domestic air travel is concerned, Qantas (<www.qantas.com.au>) is the major player, but you should be able to find cheaper fares – and some bargains – with the budget airlines, Virgin Blue (<www.virginblue.com.au>), Jetstar (<www.jetstar.com>) and Tiger Air (<www.tigerairways.com>). International passengers may be entitled to discounted travel within Australia, depending on the airline they arrive on and their fare type.

On the ground, train travel can be competitive for shorter distances, and budget long-distance coach operations abound.

In 2009, the cost of a litre of petrol (gasoline) was approximately A$1.20 – more expensive than in the US but cheaper than in the majority of European countries.

C

CAMPING (see also CAR HIRE and NATIONAL PARKS)

Australians are avid campers, and you'll find campsites dotted all over the areas frequented by tourists. The sites tend to be jam-packed at school holiday times. They have at least the basic amenities, and in some cases much more in the way of comfort. Apart from roomy tents with lights and floors, some installations have caravans (trailers) or cabins for rent. Showers, toilets, laundry facilities and barbecue grills are commonly available.

The national parks generally have well-organised camping facilities; to camp beyond the designated zone you must ask the rangers for permission. There are coach tours for campers, or you can rent a camper van or motorhome by the day or week.

CAR HIRE (see also DRIVING)

For seeing the Australian countryside at your own pace, there's no substitute for a car. Brisk competition among the international and local car hire companies means you can often find economical rates or special deals, for instance unlimited mileage or weekend discounts. Rates are considerably higher if you drive in remote country areas. In general, it's worth shopping around. But be careful – some cheap companies impose a metropolitan limit on vehicles. Check first, as your insurance won't be valid outside the designated area.

In busy locations you can hire anything from a super-economy model or a four-wheel-drive vehicle to a limousine with or without chauffeur. Campervans and caravans are available, though many are reserved well in advance for school holiday periods.

To hire a car you'll need a current Australian, overseas or International Driving Licence. The minimum age is 21, or in some cases 25. Third-party insurance is automatically included, and for an additional fee you can also sign up for collision damage waiver and personal accident insurance.

You can pick up a car in one city and return it elsewhere. Interstate arrangements are commonly available from the big firms like Avis <www.avis.com/au>, Hertz <www.hertz.com.au>, Thrifty <www. thrifty.com.au> and Budget <www.budget.com.au>, which also have offices at airports.

CLIMATE

Travellers from the Northern Hemisphere find Australia's seasons upside down: winter runs from June to August and Christmas comes in summertime. But it's much more complicated than that, for Australia covers so much ground, from the tropics to the temperate zone.

From November to March it's mostly hot, or at least quite warm, everywhere. In the north this period brings high humidity and rain, which can wash out roads and otherwise spoil holiday plans. In the south the nights, at least, are mild. April to September is generally ideal in the tropics and central Australia – clear and warm. Occasional rain refreshes the south, with snow in the southern mountains.

For your guidance, the table below gives the average daily maximum and minimum temperatures in degrees Fahrenheit. (Minimum temperatures are measured just before sunrise, maximum temperatures in the afternoon.)

°F		J	F	M	A	M	J	J	A	S	O	N	D
Sydney	max.	79	77	77	72	66	63	61	63	68	72	75	77
	min.	64	64	63	59	52	48	46	48	52	55	59	63
Brisbane	max.	84	84	82	79	73	71	68	72	75	79	82	84
	min.	69	68	66	61	55	52	48	50	55	61	64	63
Alice Springs	max.	99	97	91	84	73	68	66	72	79	88	93	95
	min.	72	71	64	57	48	43	41	45	50	59	64	68
Perth	max.	86	86	82	75	71	64	63	64	66	71	77	81
	min.	64	64	63	57	54	50	48	48	50	52	59	61

...and the same in degrees Celsius:

°C		J	F	M	A	M	J	J	A	S	O	N	D
Sydney	max.	26	25	25	22	19	17	16	17	20	22	24	25
	min.	18	18	17	15	11	9	8	9	11	13	15	17
Brisbane	max.	29	29	28	26	23	21	20	22	24	26	28	29
	min.	21	20	19	16	13	11	9	10	13	16	18	17
Alice Springs	max.	37	36	33	29	23	20	19	22	26	31	34	35
	min.	22	21	18	14	9	6	5	7	10	15	18	20
Perth	max.	30	30	28	24	21	18	17	18	19	21	25	27
	min.	18	18	17	14	12	10	9	9	10	11	14	16

By way of regional superlatives, Darwin is the state capital with the highest average hours of sunshine, but it also gets the most rain. Adelaide has the lowest average rainfall of all capital cities. Far to the south, Hobart is the coolest capital; its climate is similar to that of Britain. But statistics indicate that the cities of Australia bask in more sunshine than any others in the world.

CLOTHING

A sweater may come in handy, even in summer. After a hot day in the sun, the evening breeze can seem chilly. A light raincoat will serve in any season. Anywhere you go you'll need comfortable walking shoes. Because of the strong sun, a hat is advisable.

While Sydneysiders dress casually at weekends (shorts, a short-sleeved shirt or T-shirt and trainers or sandals are perfect), business attire can be surprisingly conservative. Visit any popular downtown pub in Sydney or Melbourne at lunchtime on a summer weekday and you encounter hundreds of men in dark blue suits and ties, trying to cope with the sweltering heat. Sydney has yet to adapt fully to its climate and adopt the open-necked informality seen in many warm countries. Restaurants have dropped the requirement for men to wear jacket and tie, but some establishments may refuse customers wearing T-shirts, tank tops or ripped jeans. Entering clubs generally requires a collared shirt and covered shoes – no trainers, thongs (flip-flops) or sandals.

COMPLAINTS

If you think you've been overcharged or unfairly dealt with, the personal approach can be effective in plain-talking Australia. If not, consider contacting the travel agency that made the booking. Failing that, phone or write to the Department of Fair Trading or Department of Consumer Affairs in the Australian state or territory concerned. Their contact details are listed in the phone book's White Pages, up front in the government section.

CRIME AND SAFETY (see also EMERGENCIES)

As in most countries, it's wise to take precautions against burglary and petty theft. Check your valuables into the hotel's safe deposit box. Lock your room and your car. Be alert for pickpockets on crowded buses and in the markets.

Overall, Australia is a safe place. Sydney's murder rate (1 per 100,000 citizens) is low by world standards and the city, Australia's biggest, has a relatively low crime rate. The same is true of other Australian cities, although muggings and fights are not unknown. It's best to avoid city parks after dark, particularly if on your own. Anti-drug laws vary greatly from state to state. Possession of small amounts of cannabis for personal use is generally either overlooked or dealt with by a fine. Narcotics are treated much more severely.

CUSTOMS AND ENTRY REQUIREMENTS

Australia requires all visitors to hold a visa. Citizens of New Zealand (which has close links with Australia) receive an automatic electronic visa when they present their passports at the Immigration desk.

Australia's Electronic Travel Authority (ETA) allows travel agents and airlines to issue a visa electronically to visitors at the time of flight booking in their home countries. You can also apply yourself via the internet at <www.eta.immi.gov.au>. People visiting friends or relatives or just coming as tourists and wishing to stay for up to three months should apply for the Visitor ETA, which costs A$20. Those making a business visit of less than three months should apply for a Short Validity Business ETA.

ETAs are currently available to citizens of 30 or so countries, including Canada, Denmark, Finland, France, Germany, Greece, Ireland, Italy, Japan, Malaysia, the Netherlands, Norway, Portugal, Singapore, Spain, Sweden, Switzerland, the UK and the US. For the full list, see the website of the Department of Immigration and Multicultural Affairs (<www.immi.gov.au>).

If you wish to extend your stay beyond three months, you will need to apply to the department for a visa extension, which costs at least $A200. See the department's web site for contact details.

If you are not a passport holder of one of the ETA-approved countries above, or wish to stay longer than three months, you should apply for a Tourist Visa, valid for up to six months. You can download a visa application form from the department's website. An application fee is payable.

Australia operates reciprocal working holiday programmes with countries, including Canada, Denmark, France, Germany, Ireland, Italy, Japan, Korea, Malta, the Netherlands, Norway, Sweden, and the UK, for applicants between 18 and 30, either single or married without children. Working holiday visas allow recipients to work for up to three months at a time, over a one-year period.

On arrival in Australia, you may have to show your return or onward ticket, and prove that you have sufficient funds for your stay. On entry, each person may take into Australia duty-free up to 2.25 litres (about ½ gallon) of alcohol and 250 cigarettes or 250g (9oz) of tobacco.

D

DRIVING (see also CAR HIRE)

Road conditions. Australian roads are good considering the size of the country and the challenges of distance, terrain and climate. Freeways link populous regions, but most country roads are two-lane highways, which can be crowded at busy times. Outback roads are often unpaved and, in the tropical north, can be impassable during the wet season.

Rules and regulations. Australians drive on the left – which means the steering wheel is on the right, and you overtake on the right. Drivers and passengers must wear seat belts. (The exception is buses, although many of them feature seat belts as an option.) Car-hire companies can supply suitable child restraints, boosters and baby seats at an extra charge.

A tourist may drive in Australia on a valid overseas licence for the same class of vehicle. Licences must always be carried when driving. If the licence is in a language other than English, the visitor must carry a translation with the licence. An International Driver's Permit must be accompanied by a valid national driver's licence.

The speed limit in cities and towns is generally 60kph (about 35mph), but many local and suburban roads have a 50kph (about 40mph) speed limit. Outside built-up areas the speed limit is generally either 100kph or 110kph (about 70mph). Speed limits are rigorously enforced by the police.

Throughout Australia, police make random checks for drugs or alcohol, using breath tests. The limit on alcohol in the blood is 0.05, meaning in practice that two or three glasses of wine or two or three half-pint glasses of beer in an hour will take you to the limit. In New South Wales, if you are under 25 and in your first three years of driving, you must be under 0.02, which doesn't allow you to drink at all. In any state, being over the limit means an automatic hefty fine.

Outback driving. Check thoroughly the condition of your car and be sure you have a spare tyre and plenty of drinking water. Find out about the fuel situation in advance and always be sure to leave word as to your destination and anticipated arrival time. Fill up the fuel tank at every opportunity, as the next station may be a few hundred kilometres away. Some dirt roads are so smooth you may be tempted to speed, but conditions can change abruptly. Be cautious when you encounter a 'road train' – a high-powered truck towing three or four trailers along the highway at speed. Pass only with the greatest of care.

Parking. Heavy traffic and parking problems afflict some downtown areas. Parking meters and 'no standing' zones are everywhere, so be careful where you leave the car.

If you need help. The Australian Automobile Association <www.aaa.asn.au> is a national body that maintains links with similar organisations worldwide. Many state automobile associations have reciprocal arrangements with similar organisations overseas, so bring proof of your membership.

New South Wales: NMRA, 388 George Street, Sydney, NSW 2000; tel: (02) 8741 6000; <www.mynrma.com.au>.

Victoria: RACV, 550 Princes Highway, Noble Park, Victoria 3174; tel: (03) 9790 2211; <www.racv.com.au>.

Queensland: RACQ, 300 St Paul's Terrace, Fortitude Valley, QLD 4006; tel: (07) 3361 2444; <www.racq.com.au>.

South Australia: RAA, 55 Hindmarsh Square, Adelaide, SA 5000; tel: (08) 8202 4600; <www.raa.net>.

Tasmania: RACT, Corner of Patrick and Murray Streets, Hobart, TAS 7000; tel: (02) 6232 6300; <www.ract.com.au>.

Western Australia: RACWA, 832 Wellington Street, West Perth WA 6000; tel: (08) 9436 44444; <www.rac.com.au>.

Northern Territory: AANT, 79-81 Smith Street, Darwin, NT 0800; tel: (08) 8981 3837; <www.aant.com.au>.

Fuel. Some filling stations are open only during normal shopping hours, so you may have to ask where after-hours service is available. Petrol (gasoline) in Australia comes in regular and premium grades, leaded and unleaded, and is sold by the litre. Most stations are self-service and accept international credit cards.

Road signs. Signs are generally good, especially along heavily used roads. All distances are measured in kilometres. White-on-brown direction signs signal tourist attractions and natural wonders. To drive into the centre of any city, simply follow the signs marked 'City'. Leaving a city is less straightforward: exit routes are often signposted with the assumption that every driver has local experience, so you may require a good map. Most road signs are the standard international pictographs, but some are unique to Australia, such as silhouette images of kangaroos or wombats, warning that you may encounter these animals crossing the road. Some signs use words, such as:

Crest steep	hilltop limiting visibility
Cyclist hazard	dangerous for cyclists
Dip	severe depression in road surface
Hump	bump or speed obstacle
Safety ramp	uphill escape lane from steep downhill road

E

ELECTRICITY

The standard throughout Australia is 230–250 volt, 50-cycle AC. Three-pronged plugs, in the shape of a bird's footprint, are universal. They are the same as in New Zealand and many Pacific countries. If you are from elsewhere, you will need an adapter. Many hotel rooms also have 110-volt outlets for razors and small appliances.

EMBASSIES/CONSULATES/HIGH COMMISSIONS

The embassies or high commissions of about 70 countries are established in Canberra, the national capital. They have consular sections dealing with passport renewal, visas and other formalities. Some of them run consular sections in Sydney and other cities, as well. To find the address of your consulate, look in the white pages of the telephone directory under 'Consuls', or in the Yellow Pages under 'Consulates and Legations'.

Here are some of the Canberra embassies and high commissions:

British High Commission: Commonwealth Avenue, Yarralumla, ACT 2600; tel: (02) 6270 6666; <www.britaus.net>. **Consular Section (Passports and Visas):** Piccadilly House, 39 Brindabella Circuit, Canberra Airport, ACT 2609; tel: (1902) 941 555 (Information line).

Canadian High Commission: Commonwealth Avenue, Yarralumla, ACT 2600; tel: (02) 6270 4000.

Irish Embassy: 20 Arkana Street, Yarralumla, ACT 2600; tel: (02) 6273 3022.

Japanese Embassy: 112 Empire Circuit, Yarralumla, ACT 2600; tel: (02) 6273 3244.

New Zealand High Commission: Commonwealth Avenue, Yarralumla, ACT 2600; tel: (02) 6270 4211.

South Africa High Commission: Corner of State Circle and Rhodes Place, Yarralumla, ACT 2600; tel: (02) 6272 7300.

United States Embassy: Moonah Place, Yarralumla, ACT 2600; tel: (02) 6214 5600.

EMERGENCIES

Ambulance/Fire/Police: dial 000.

The 000 number – free from public telephones – is in service in all cities and most towns. You can also dial 112 if using a mobile phone.

In the big cities there are round-the-clock dental emergency services as well as hospital emergency wards.

G

GAY AND LESBIAN TRAVELLERS

Sydney's popular Gay and Lesbian Mardi Gras has helped make Sydney – and Australia – a popular destination for gay and lesbian travellers. Some tour operators, travel agents and hotels specialise in catering for a gay and lesbian clientele. Australian cities are generally tolerant towards gay and lesbian travellers but prejudice tends to increase in more remote, country areas. Homosexual acts are legal in all states. Sydney is one of the world's major gay cities, sometimes called 'the gay capital of the Southern Hemisphere'. Sydney's main gay precinct is Oxford Street (sometimes called 'the Golden Mile') and the surrounding Darlinghurst and Surry Hills areas, with another precinct in King Street, Newtown.

GETTING TO AUSTRALIA

By air. Flights from Asia, North America and Europe serve international airports around Australia, including Sydney, Cairns or Melbourne, and you can also fly directly to Darwin, Perth, Brisbane or Adelaide from many international points. Sydney's airport is by far the busiest one in the country. Sydney (and other Australian airports) have particularly high volumes of traffic around the Christmas holiday period, which coincides with the Australian midsummer. Fares are generally at their highest then, and flights are heavily booked in both directions, so it's best to avoid midsummer travel if you are on a budget.

Australia is included in several round-the-world fare constructions – arrangements between two or more airlines which allow passengers to travel globally at bargain rates, provided they complete their journeys within a year and don't backtrack.

Flight times to Sydney (approximate) are as follows: London–Sydney 21 hours, New York–Sydney 22 hours, Los Angeles–Sydney 15 hours. You can usually break the flight for a day or two at one of the stops along the way; in most cases this doesn't affect the price of the air ticket.

By sea. No passenger liners operate to or from Australia any more, but some Australian ports, notably Sydney and Cairns, feature in the itineraries of cruise ships. You can fly to locales like Bali or Singapore and embark on the cruise liner there, sail to Australia, then fly home from any Australian city, or resume the cruise at another port. It tends to be an involved process, however. Travel agents have cruise line schedules and brochures.

GUIDES AND TOURS

Tour companies offer a broad choice of excursions, from a day-trip to Canberra to long-haul journeys into the Outback. There are also local walking tours and tours for cyclists, wildlife-lovers and others catering for special interests.

H

HEALTH AND MEDICAL CARE

Standards of hygiene in Australia are high, particularly in food preparation. Doctors and dentists are proficient and hospitals well-equipped. If you fall ill, your hotel can call a doctor or refer you to one, or you can ask your embassy, high commission or consulate for a list of approved doctors.

You should take out health insurance before departure to cover your stay in Australia. Also ensure that you have personal insurance or travel insurance with a comprehensive health component to cover the possibility of illness or accident.

Medicare, Australia's national health insurance, covers visitors from New Zealand, the UK, Ireland, Malta, Sweden, Italy, Finland, Norway and the Netherlands. To be eligible, contact your national health programme before travelling to Australia to ensure that you have the correct documents should you need to enrol at a Medicare office (you can enrol before or after you receive treatment). The agreement provides urgent treatment but doesn't cover elective surgery, dental care, ambulance services or illness arising en route to Australia. The agreements do not cover repatriation in the case of illness or injury.

You are allowed to bring 'reasonable quantities' of prescribed, non-narcotic medications. All should be clearly labelled and identifiable. For large quantities, bring a doctor's certificate to produce to Customs if necessary. All medication must be carried in personal hand luggage. Local chemists can fill most prescriptions – which must be written by an Australian-registered doctor.

Health hazards exist on the seas and in the countryside, starting with the threat of too much sun. High-factor sun-screen cream is essential if exposed, even on cloudy days.

Poisonous spiders live in Australia. The dark, bulbous, Sydney funnelweb is one of the world's most lethal and aggressive types of spider. Although its bites are rare (about 10 victims a year), they require immediate medical attention to stave off coma and death. Catch the spider for identification if you can. Other poisonous spiders include the redback, the eastern mouse spider and the white-tail.

Shark attacks are also rare, but one is too many and may well be your last. Swim between the flags and heed shark alarms.

In certain seasons and areas, the bluebottle **jellyfish** (also called Portuguese-man-of-war) may be encountered. Its sting is painful but can be treated. Far more dangerous are the box jellyfish (seawasp) and the irukandji jellyish, which are found in tropical waters from about October to April. A sting from either species can be fatal. Never disregard warning signs on beaches. In the north of Australia, **saltwater crocodiles** can be a menace to swimmers. Again, obey the signs. Other marine hazards include the stonefish and the blue-ringed octopus. Both can cause death.

Several of the world's deadliest **snakes**, including the brown snake, tiger snake, taipan and death adder, are indigenous to Australia. You are unlikely to encounter them in built-up areas. The inland taipan, or fierce snake, has the most potent venom in the world, but is restricted to sparsely populated areas of southwest Queensland, so few people are bitten. If you are bitten by any snake, seek immediate medical attention.

The good news is that you can drink water from taps anywhere unless specifically marked otherwise. In the Outback, warnings may read 'Bore water', 'Non-potable' or 'Not for drinking'.

HITCH-HIKING

It's better not to hitch-hike, which is banned on freeways and throughout the whole state of Queensland. Even where it is tolerated, it can be risky. Some city hostels feature notice boards where people driving interstate can advertise for a travelling companion to share costs. That way, you at least get to meet the person you might travel with. Cut-rate bus travel is a safer and better option.

HOLIDAYS

1 January	New Year's Day
26 January	Australia Day
25 April	Anzac Day
25 December	Christmas Day
26 December	Boxing Day
Moveable dates	Good Friday, Easter, Easter Monday, Queen's Birthday

Additional public holidays are celebrated only in certain states, while other holidays are observed at different times in different states. School holidays arrive four times a year; the longest one is in the summer through the latter part of December and all of January, tending to crowd hotels and tourist attractions.

L

LANGUAGE

Australian is spoken everywhere – that is to say, English with a distinctive accent. The vernacular is sometimes called 'Strine', which is the way the word 'Australian' sounds in an extreme Australian pronunciation. While educated and cultivated Australians tend to speak in more neutral accents, Strine in the backblocks can sound to an American ear like a profound Cockney intonation piped through the nose. Here are a few interesting Australian terms and colloquialisms:

ankle-biter	young child
arvo	afternoon
back of Bourke	far Outback
beaut	(from beautiful) very good, fantastic
billabong	waterhole in a semi-dry river
bitser	mongrel (bits of this and bits of that)
bludger	sponger, tightwad, lazy person
bonzer	terrific
boomer	huge kangaroo
bunyip	akin to Australia's yeti or Bigfoot
cask	box of cheap wine
chook	chicken
cossie	swimming costume
crook	broken, sick, no good
dag	mild term for fool or uncool person
damper	unleavened bread, staple of bush tucker
dinkie die	the truth
dinkum	genuine or honest
drongo	idiot
dunny	toilet

esky	cooler
fair enough	agreed, acceptable
galah	fool (after the parrot of the same name)
greenie	conservationist
grizzle	complain
heart starter	first drink of the day
hoon	loudmouth, reckless driver
jackaroo	male worker on an outback station
jillaroo	female worker on an outback station
jumbuck	lamb
kark it	to die
larrikin	mischievous person
lob	arrive ('to lob in')
lurk	racket or illegal scheme
middy	285ml/10oz glass of beer (in NSW)
nervy	nervous attack ('to chuck a nervy')
ocker	bumpkin, loudmouth
pokie	slot machine
ripper	very good
roo	kangaroo
rooted	exhausted
scunge	dirty, untidy person
she'll be apples	it'll be fine
shoot through	leave unexpectedly, escape
shout	to buy a round of drinks
snags	sausages
stubby	small bottle of beer
tinnie or tube	can of beer
ute	pick-up truck
wowser	kiljoy, prude
yabber	chatter
yakka	work

LAUNDRY AND DRY CLEANING

Hotels and motels usually offer one-day laundry and dry cleaning service for guests, but it can be expensive. Ask the receptionist or maid. Many hotels and motels also have launderette facilities.

M

MAPS

State and local tourist offices give away useful maps of their areas. If you need more detailed maps, check at newsstands and bookshops. Car hire companies often supply free city directories showing each street and place of interest. If you're driving beyond the cities you'll want to buy an up-to-date road map of the region. On the internet, see <www.whereis.com.au>.

MEDIA

More than 500 newspapers are published in Australia, ranging from big-city dailies like the *Sydney Morning Herald* and *The Age* of Melbourne to small-circulation weeklies. Among the latter are local periodicals aimed at the various immigrant communities, published in Dutch, French, German, Greek, Italian and other languages. In the bigger cities, specialist newsstands sell airmail copies of newspapers from London, Rome, New York and Paris, in addition to weekly and monthly American and European magazines. The UK *Guardian Weekly* is now printed in Sydney.

CNN and other satellite news services are available at most international-standard hotels, and you may be able to read your hometown paper on the Internet at one of an Internet café.

MONEY

Australian currency is decimal, with the dollar the basic unit (100 cents to one dollar). Notes come in A$100, A$50, A$20, A$10 and A$5 denominations. Coins come in 5c, 10c, 20c, 50c, A$1 and A$2 denominations. There being no 1c or 2c coins, cash transactions are rounded up or down to the nearest 5c, so an item priced at A$11.99 will cost you A$12 and something priced at A$11.96 will cost you A$11.95. Non-cash transactions, such as those using a credit card, are not subject to rounding.

As for **credit cards**, MasterCard and Visa are widely accepted (Diners Club and American Express less so), but you may have problems with them in smaller towns and country areas and small shops. Some shops impose a small surcharge for credit card purchases.

All international airports in Australia provide **currency exchange** facilities, and foreign notes or travellers' cheques can be converted at most banks. Cash travellers' cheques at banks or larger hotels (despite the charges), as it may be difficult elsewhere. Know that Australian banks charge for just about everything these days.

ATM machines are widespread. You should be able to obtain cash directly in this way using your credit/debit card and with the same PIN number you use at home.

N

NATIONAL PARKS

The vast majority of Australia's national parks are run by state- or territory-based authorities. Their details are:

ACT: National Parks and Wildlife Service, 6 Rutledge Street, Queanbeyan ACT 2620; tel: (02) 6299 2929.

New South Wales: National Parks and Wildlife Service, Level 14, 59–61 Goulburn Street, Sydney NSW 2000; tel: 1300 361 967; <www.nationalparks.nsw.gov.au>.

Queensland: Parks and Wildlife Service, 160 Ann Street, Brisbane QLD 4000; tel: 13 13 04; <www.epa.qld.gov.au/parks_and_forests>.

Northern Territory: Parks and Wildlife Service of Northern Territory, PO Box 496, Goyder Centre, 25 Chung Wah Terrace, Palmerston, NT 0830; tel: (08) 8999 4555; <http://nt.gov.au/nreta/parks>.

Western Australia: Conservation and Land Management (CALM), Hackett Drive, Crawley, WA 6009; tel: (08) 9442 0300; <www.calm.wa.gov.au>.

South Australia: Dept for Environment and Heritage, GPO Box 1047, Adelaide, SA 5001; tel: (08) 8204 1910; <www.parks.sa.gov.au>.

Victoria: Parks Victoria, Level 10, 535 Bourke Street, Melbourne, Victoria 3000; tel: (03) 8627 4699; <www.parkweb.vic.gov.au>.

Tasmania: Parks and Wildlife Service Tasmania, GPO Box 1751, Hobart, Tasmania, 7001; tel: 1300 135 513; <www.parks.tas.gov.au>.

A small number of parks, including Kakadu and Uluru–Kata Tjuta national parks, are managed by the federal government: **Australian Department of the Environment, Water, Heritage and the Arts:** <www.environment.gov.au>.

For information on the Great Barrier Reef Marine Park, contact: **Great Barrier Reef Marine Park Authority:** <www.gbrmpa.gov.au>.

OPENING HOURS

Banks generally open from 9.30am to 4pm Monday to Thursday and from 9.30am to 5pm on Fridays. In big cities, selected banking facilities may be available on Saturday morning, but don't rely on it.

General **office hours** are 9am to 5pm, Monday to Friday; **post offices** follow the same hours. Stamps are often available at the front desks of hotels and at some retail outlets, usually newsagents.

Shopping: Most shops close at 5 or 5.30pm on weekdays. In most towns, shops have one (or sometimes two) late shopping nights a week, when stores stay open to 9 or 9.30 pm. This is usually on Thursday or Friday. Sunday trading is becoming more common in larger cities, and some stores operate 24 hours a day.

Bars, pubs and hotels: Licensing hours vary by state, but a typical schedule would be 10am–11pm or midnight Monday to Saturday, with most pubs open by noon on Sundays as well, closing at 10pm.

P

POLICE

Each state operates its own police force, covering both urban and rural areas. The federal police force has jurisdiction over government property, including airports.

The police emergency telephone number is 000.

POST OFFICES

Australia's post offices are signposted 'Australia Post'. Most branches adhere to a 9am–5pm schedule Monday to Friday, though big-city General Post Offices often remain open for extended hours.

Postcards and letters to the US or Europe cost A$1.95, and international aerograms cost $1.05 cents, whatever their destination. Local letters cost 50 cents. Mailboxes throughout Australia are red, with an Australia Post logo. Most post offices have fax facilities, as do hotels. Internet cafés exist in all Australian cities and are spreading rapidly in small centres, too.

PUBLIC TRANSPORT

This is highly developed in most Australian cities, with buses and trains being the most common forms. Sydney Airport is now connected directly to the city by rail.

Sydney has its quirky monorail that links the central city to Darling Harbour, and also has a light rail system from Central Station to Chinatown, the Fish Markets and beyond. A fine fleet of ferries is concentrated at Circular Quay. The ferries provide cheap outings for sightseers to Manly, Watsons Bay, Cremorne Point, Neutral Bay or Taronga Zoo.

Melbourne's trams are not only decorative – they're a vital part of city transport. The gold-and-burgundy-coloured City Circle tram is free. In Adelaide, trams run to Glenelg, and the O-Bahn ('bullet bus') provides highly efficient transport to outer suburbs.

R

RELIGION

The major religion in Australia is Christianity. Of the non-Christian faiths, Buddhists are the largest group, followed by Muslims, Hindus and Jews. To find the church of your choice, check at your hotel desk or look in the Yellow Pages of the phone directory under 'Churches and Synagogues'. Most of the major religions will be represented.

T

TAX REFUNDS

A Goods and Services Tax (GST) of 10 percent applies to most purchases. The Tourist Refund Scheme (TRS) allows overseas visitors to claim a limited GST refund as they clear customs. To qualify for the TRS you need to have spent at least A$300 (including GST), either from the same store (at the one time or over several occasions – but a single tax invoice for all the goods must be provided), or from several stores, no more than 30 days before you leave Australia. You must also take the goods with you as carry-on luggage.

TELEPHONES

Australia's country code is 61. This is followed by a city code, generally 2 for NSW or the ACT, 3 for Victoria and Tasmania, 7 for Queensland and 8 for the Northern Territory, South Australia or Western Australia.

Australia's telephone network is sophisticated; you can dial anywhere in the country from almost any phone, even in the Outback, and expect a loud and clear line. Many hotel rooms have phones from which you can dial cross-Australia (STD) or internationally (IDD). Some hotels add a surcharge to your telephone bill.

The minimum cost of a local public payphone call is 50c. Long-distance calls within Australia (STD) and International Direct Dialing

(IDD) calls can be made on Telstra public payphones. Check with the operator for these charges as they vary for distances and the time of day of the call. Public payphones accept most coins and Phonecards. A Phonecard is a pre-paid card for use in public payphones to make local, STD and IDD calls. Phonecards are sold at newsagents, post offices and other shops, and come in denominations of A$5, A$10 and A$20. The Telstra PhoneAway pre-paid card enables you to use virtually any phone in Australia – home and office phones, mobile phones, hotel and payphones – all call costs are charged against the card. If you need assistance, help is available in seven languages.

Creditphones accept most major credit cards such as Amex, Visa and MasterCard and can be found at international and domestic airports, central-city locations and many hotels. To make a reverse-charge (collect) call, phone the International Operator, tel: 1225.

Telephone directories give instructions on dialling and details on emergency and other services. To reach an overseas number, dial 0011, then the country code of the destination, the area code and the local number.

TIME ZONES

Australia has three time zones: Eastern Standard Time (EST), which operates in New South Wales, Australian Capital Territory, Victoria, Tasmania and Queensland; Central Standard Time (CST) in South Australia and Northern Territory (and in the NSW Outback town of Broken Hill); and Western Standard Time (WST) in Western Australia.

CST is 30 minutes behind EST, while WST is two hours behind EST. Daylight saving (setting the clocks forward an hour) operates in all states and territories, except Queensland and the Northern Territory, from the beginning of October through to the first week in April.

Sydney is on EST, which is 10 hours ahead of Greenwich Mean Time and 15 hours ahead of New York. Time differences between Australia's zones and other countries vary seasonally as daylight saving is switched on and off by Australia or the other country. So when it's winter in the northern hemisphere, and daylight saving is operating in New South Wales, the time difference between London and Sydney is 11 hours. But during British Summertime, when Sydney is on EST, it's only nine hours. One way to get it right is to access <www.whitepages.com.au> and use the world time calculator under 'Helpful Info'.

TIPPING

Tipping is discretionary, and nobody's livelihood depends on tipping. It is not customary to tip taxi drivers, porters at airports or hairdressers, although you may do so if you wish. Porters have set charges at railway terminals, but not at hotels. Hotels and restaurants do not usually add service charges to accounts, although some restaurants and cafés add a 10 percent surcharge for service on public holidays. In restaurants, patrons usually tip food and drink waiters up to 10 percent, but only if service is good. (If you are ecstatic about the service, make it 15 percent.) Tipping is an optional gratuity for good service. It has not developed into a means of subsidising wages. If service is poor or a waiter is surly or impolite, don't tip.

TOILETS

'Dunny' is the Aussie slang term for toilet, but 'washroom', 'restrooms', 'loos', 'ladies' or 'gents' are all understood. Public toilets are often locked after certain hours, but you can generally use the facilities in any pub or cinema complex without needing to buy a drink or a movie ticket, and department store toilets are always handy.

TOURIST INFORMATION

To obtain tourist information before you leave home, access the website of Tourism Australia <www.australia.com> or contact them in your country of residence or at their Australian head office: Level 18, Darling Park, Tower 2, 201 Sussex Street, Sydney NSW 2000, Australia; tel: (02) 9360 1111; fax: (02) 9331 6469.

Overseas Tourism Australia offices:

UK: Australia Centre, Australia House, 6th Floor, Melbourne Place, The Strand, London WC2B 4LG; tel: (020) 7438 4601; fax: (020) 7240 6690.

US: 6100 Center Drive, Suite 1150, Los Angeles CA 90045; tel: (310) 695 3200; fax: (310) 695 3201.

New Zealand: Level 3, 125 The Strand, Parnell, Auckland 1; tel: (09) 915 2826; fax: (09) 307 3117.

State tourist offices in Australia are:

Canberra and Region Visitors Centre: 330 Northbourne Avenue, Dickson, ACT 2602; tel: 1300 554 114; fax: (02) 6205 0776.

Sydney Visitor Centre: Cnr Argyle and Playfair streets, The Rocks, Sydney NSW 2000; tel: 1800 067 676 or (02) 9240 8788.

Tourism Top End: 6 Bennett Street (Cnr Bennett and Smith Streets), Darwin NT 0800; tel: 1300 138 886 or (08) 8980 6000.

South Australia Visitors Centre: 18 King William Street, Adelaide SA 5000; tel: 1300-655 276; fax: (08) 8303 2249.

Melbourne Visitor Centre: Federation Square, Cnr Swanston and Flinders Streets, Melbourne; tel: 13 28 42.

Western Australian Visitor Centre: Albert Facey House, Forrest Place, Perth; tel: 1300 361 351 or (08) 9483 1111; fax: (08) 9481 0190.

Even in the smallest town you will find an outlet distributing local tourist information and advice free of charge. Look for the international 'i' sign.

W

WEBSITES

Tourism Australia: **www.australia.com**
Travel Online: **www.travelonline.com**
Australian Travel and Tourism: **www.atn.com.au**
Western Australian Tourism: **www.westernaustralia.com**

Northern Territory Tourist Commission: **http://en.travelnt.com**

Tourism Tasmania: **www.discovertasmania.com.au**

Tourism Victoria: **www.visitvictoria.com**

Tourism New South Wales: **www.visitnsw.com.au**

South Australian Tourist Commission: **www.southaustralia.com**

Tourism Queensland: **www.queenslandholidays.com**

Canberra Tourism: **www.visitcanberra.com.au**

Visas: **www.immi.gov.au** or **www.eta.immi.gov.au**

Latest currency exchange rates: **www.xe.net**

Department of Environment, Water, Heritage and the Arts: **www. deh.gov.au**

Sydney Morning Herald: **www.smh.com.au**

Melbourne *Age*: **www.theage.com.au**

WEIGHTS AND MEASURES

Australia moved to the metric system in the 1970s. Old-timers may still refer to distances in miles, but generally the abandonment of British Imperial measures has taken total effect.

Y

YOUTH HOSTELS

There are two types of hostel accommodation: privately-owned backpacker hostels and YHA (Youth Hostels Association) Hostels. Both provide self-catering accommodation from about A\$30 a night.

The Australian YHA is Australia's largest budget accommodation network, with more than 140 hostels in a wide range of locations. They are open to all ages and offer sleeping, self-catering kitchens and common rooms where you'll meet fellow travellers.

You can join the YHA in your own country or in Australia. Contact the YHA (422 Kent Street, Sydney, NSW 2001; tel: (02) 9261 1111; <www.yha.com.au>) for a free information pack giving membership details and a list of hostels.

INDEX

Berlitz pocket guide

Australia

Twelfth Edition 2008
Reprinted 2011

Written by Ken Bernstein
Updated by John Mapps
Edited by Anna Tyler and John Mapps
Series Editor: Tom Stainer

Photography credits
Apa Photo Agency 175; Australian Tourist Board 9, 101, 111, 112, 114, 121, 123, 138, 141, 151; Jon Davison 6, 13, 21, 23, 24, 28, 33, 34, 50, 53, 56, 59, 60, 69, 78, 85, 99, 103, 107, 108, 118, 125, 137, 142, 147, 153, 155, 159, 161, 184, 191, 212; Jerry Dennis 8, 10, 11, 18, 19, 31, 38–9, 41, 42, 44, 46, 47, 65, 72, 77, 80, 81, 83, 84, 88, 91, 92, 94, 95, 97, 100, 163, 164, 167, 168, 171, 173, 174, 177, 178, 180, 181, 183, 187, 189, 196, 198, 199, 204, 207, 211, 215, 223; Michael Gebicki 15, 66; Glyn Genin 27, 37, 40, 43, 49, 57, 63, 126, 128, 129, 131, 132, 133, 134, 193, 201, 219, 220; Kevin Hamdorf/Apa 208; Claude Hüber 116–7, 160; Photolibrary 104; Steven Pohlner 144, 217; Andrew Tauber 30; Tourism New South Wales 48, 55, 75, 221; Tourism Queensland 17, 87, 194; Tourism South Australia 148, 156; John Van Hasselt/Corbis 203.
Cover picture: Theo Allofs/zefa/Corbis

Contact us

At Berlitz we strive to keep our guides as accurate and up to date as possible, but if you find anything that has changed, or if you have any suggestions on ways to improve this guide, then we would be delighted to hear from you.

Berlitz Publishing, PO Box 7910, London SE1 1WE, England.
email: berlitz@apaguide.co.uk
www.berlitzpublishing.com